CHINA HANDBOOK

D0401753

HISTORY

Compiled by
the *China Handbook* Editorial Committee

Translated by
Dun J. Li

FOREIGN LANGUAGES PRESS BEIJING

First Edition 1982

ISBN 0-8351-0985-2

Published by Foreign Languages Press
24 Baiwanzhuang Road, Beijing, China

Printed by Foreign Languages Printing House
19 West Chegongzhuang Road, Beijing, China

Distributed by China Publications Centre (Guoji Shudian)
P.O. Box 399, Beijing, China

Printed in the People's Republic of China

EDITOR'S NOTE

More than 30 years have elapsed since the birth of the People's Republic of China on October 1, 1949. "What is China really like today?" many people abroad wish to know. To answer this question, we plan to compile and publish a voluminous *China Handbook*, in which we intend to introduce the New China in every field of its activities. Emphasis will be on the process of development during the past three decades, the accomplishments and the problems that still remain. The book will contain accurate statistics and related materials, all of which will be ready references for an interested reader.

To enhance the usefulness of the forthcoming volume, we plan to publish 10 major sections separately at first, so that we shall have an opportunity to take into consideration the opinions of our readers before all the composite parts are put together, revised and published as one volume. These separate sections are:

Geography
History
Politics
Economy
Education and Science
Literature and Art
Sports and Public Health
Culture
Life and Lifestyles

Tourism

Here, we wish particularly to point out the following:

First, the statistics listed in each separate book exclude those of Taiwan, unless otherwise indicated.

Second, the statistics are those compiled up to the end of 1980.

The *China Handbook* Editorial Committee

CONTENTS

CHINA, representing one of the earliest civilizations in the world, has a recorded history of about 3,600 years. It possesses rich historical documents as well as ancient relics. Like other nations, China, in its development, passed through the stages of primitive society, slave society, and feudal society. During the middle decades of the 19th century, capitalist forces of foreign countries invaded China, and China, from then on, was slowly transformed into a semi-colonial and semi-feudal society. The founding of the People's Republic in 1949 marked China's entry into the socialist stage. During the long period of historical development, the industrious, courageous, and intelligent Chinese people of all nationalities collectively created a great civilization. They made great contributions to all of mankind.

Chapter One

EARLY PERIOD (TO 1840)

1. PRIMITIVE SOCIETY (TO THE 21ST CENTURY B.C.)

Yuanmou Man, Lantian Man, and Beijing Man. China was one of the areas where man had his first beginning. From archaeological findings we know that as early as more than one million years ago, there were primitive men in this expansive area called China. The

ape-man, whose fossil was discovered in Yuanmou,
Yunnan Province — hence the term "Yuanmou Man" —
lived in that part of China approximately 1.7 million
years ago. The "Lantian Man", the ape-man whose fossil
was discovered in Lantian, Shaanxi Province, lived approximately 800,000 years ago. As far as we know at this
moment, these two groups of people were the earliest inhabitants in China. Approximately 500,000 years ago,
another group of ape-men, belonging to the species
"Beijing Man" (Peking Man), lived in Zhoukoudian,
located in the southwestern suburb of modern Beijing.
The "Beijing Man" possessed the basic characteristics of
a human being, as he walked erect on two legs. He was
able to make things and use simple tools. He knew how
to make fire and maintain it. He lived by gathering and
hunting in groups.

Yangshao Culture. A long, long period elapsed
before primitive people gradually progressed from living
in groups to living as members of a clan. Relics showing
how primitive people lived in gens communes have been
found in many parts of China. These people first lived
in matriarchal and then lived in patriarchal communes of
a gens society. The Yangshao culture, flourishing in
China some 6,000 or 7,000 years ago, was a major
representative of a matriarchal society. Then people had
already acquired the skill of making stone and bone instruments through grinding; they manufactured bows and
arrows as well as pottery. Agriculture and husbandry, in
a primitive form, had appeared. Besides, the Yangshao
people knew how to spin and weave and how to build
houses, thus beginning a more sedentary life. The Banpo
Village, unearthed near Xi'an, Shaanxi Province, represented a typical example of gens society.

**Longshan Culture: Disintegration of Primitive
Society.** Approximately 5,000 years ago, many clans
along the Huanghe (Yellow) and Changjiang (Yangtze)
rivers entered the stage of patriarchal society one after
another. The Longshan culture was a principal representative of patriarchal commune during a period when the
gens society prevailed. By then the primitive people had
already entered the later stage of the Neolithic Age.
Stone was still the major material for making tools,
though copper had already been discovered. Agricultural
products increased in quantity as well as in kind, and for
the first time the method of fermenting grain to make
wine was invented. There was a variety of domestic
animals, including horse, ox, sheep, chicken, dog, and
pig. The technology of making pottery also improved;
black pottery, white pottery, and eggshell pottery were
the innovations of this time. In the Longshan ruins were
also found such handicraft products as jade and bone
articles. All this demonstrates that production of various
kinds had increased and standard of living improved. The
progress made in the division of labour and in the exchange of commodities sped up the development of the
institution of private property and the division of society
into classes, which, in turn, precipitated the dissolution
of primitive society.

2. SLAVE SOCIETY
(21ST CENTURY TO 476 B.C.)

Slave society in China began with the Xia Dynasty.
It developed and persisted during two slave dynasties,
Yin-Shang and Western Zhou. It slowly declined and

then collapsed during the Spring and Autumn Period. It lasted approximately 1,600 years.

Xia: First Slave Regime. The Xia Dynasty (21st to 16th century B.C.) represented the first slave society in Chinese history. It began when the Great Yu abdicated in favour of his son Qi; it ended with the death of Jie, its last ruler. It lasted more than four centuries. Its major production was that of agriculture, and the centre of its activities was the western section of modern Henan Province and the southern section of modern Shanxi Province.

Shang: Dynasty of Slave Owners. During the 16th century B.C., a tribe in the lower Huanghe River valley, under its leader Tang, overthrew the Xia regime and established the Shang Dynasty (16th to 11th century B.C.). The capital of the new dynasty was Bo (modern Shangqiu, Henan Province) first; then it was moved to Yin (modern Anyang, Henan Province) during the reign of Pangeng. Great progress was made during the Shang Dynasty, politically, economically, and culturally. Relics discovered in the Yin ruins tell us a great deal about the society at that time. In the first place, governmental structure and army organization were more or less complete; walled cities also appeared. Among agricultural crops were millet, sorghum, wheat, and rice. The technology of raising silkworms and reeling silk and spinning and weaving had already been mastered, and the skill of making bronze was raised to a high level. In addition to wine vessels, bronze was used to make or manufacture weapons, items used for ceremony and ritual, food utensils, chariot parts and horse fittings, musical instruments, and tools: all of these had been found in the Yin

ruins. One square tripod, inscribed with the characters
Si Mu Wu and unearthed at Anyang, is as high as 133
centimetres and weighs as much as 875 kilogrammes. It
is grand in structure and elegant in design. It is presently
housed in the Museum of Chinese History, Beijing. As
for the written script of the Shang Dynasty, it appears
principally as oracles on tortoise shells and on shoulder
blades of oxen; it can also be found on the surface of a
bronze. Besides predicting the future, extant oracles provide information on slaves engaged in production and
domestic chores, wars, and changes in natural phenomena.
According to the Shang calendar, a year was divided into
12 months. A longer month had 30 days, and a shorter
month 29 days. A leap year had 13, instead of 12, months.
An examination of Shang tombs indicates that human
sacrifice at the time of burial was a common practice.

Western Zhou: Development of the Slave System.
In the 11th century B.C., the Zhou people (inhabiting
modern Shaanxi), under the leadership of Jifa or King
Wu, exterminated the Shang Dynasty by military force
and established a new slave regime known to historians
as Western Zhou (11th century to 770 B.C.). The capital
of the new regime was Hao, located to the southwest of
modern Xi'an, Shaanxi Province.

To strengthen its control of the country, the royal
house of Zhou, at the very beginning, adopted a system
of fiefs whereby land and people in China were awarded
to various dukes or princes. According to written record,
71 states were created in this manner; Lu, Wei, Qi, Jin,
and Yan were the largest among them. All land was supposed to belong to the king, and all slaves were compelled
to work collectively under the so-called well-field
(*jingtian*) system. The system was the principal institu-

tion regarding land usage in China's slave society that existed during both the Shang and Zhou dynasties. The Western Zhou regime employed slave labour on a massive scale and, compared to its predecessor, namely, the Shang, produced more food. There was more production of bronzes, the variety of which also increased. On some of the bronzes appear long narratives. According to one narrative, a king of Zhou awarded Yu, a noble, with 1,709 slaves.

Decline and Demise of the Slave System. In 770 B.C., the Western Zhou regime went out of existence, and the royal house of Zhou moved eastward and established its capital at Luoyi (modern Luoyang, Henan Province). From then on, the Zhou regime was known as Eastern Zhou. The era of Eastern Zhou was divided into two periods: the Spring and Autumn Period and the Warring States Period. During the Spring and Autumn Period (770-476 B.C.), the technology of smelting iron was introduced, and iron was used to make axe, plough, and other tools. The custom of using ox for ploughing had also begun. Outside the well-field system, the amount of privately owned land increased, as the system of private landownership had already come into existence. In 594 B.C., the state of Lu "collected land tax for the first time". The imposition of a land tax according to the amount of cultivated acreage indicated that public landownership in a slave society had been replaced, gradually, by private landownership in a feudal society. During the Spring and Autumn Period, the power and prestige of the royal house of Zhou slowly declined, while individual states grew in status and influence. Towards the end of this period, "private families" of ministers within each state enhanced their power and influence; as a result, the

power of the state itself gradually fell into the hands of a
new class of landlords. Slave uprisings and commoner
riots combined to speed up the demise of the slave
system.

Confucius and His Philosophy. The real name of
Confucius (551-479 B.C.) was Kong Qiu or Kong Zhongni.
He was born in Zouyi (modern Qufu, Shandong Province),
state of Lu. He was a philosopher, an educator, and the
founder of Confucianism. As the Spring and Autumn
Period marked the transition from the slave to the feudal
system, Confucius, quoting *Zhou Rites*, wanted to return
to the former that had already been destroyed. It was his
hope that the old order be re-established and the rule
by the slave-owning aristocracy be maintained. Not
surprisingly, his teachings, having been improved upon,
were later adopted by the feudal class. Nevertheless, he
made important contributions as an educator and as a
synthesizer and promoter of the ancient civilization of
China. It was reported that he had 3,000 students altogether, 72 of whom became famous. In education, he proposed "teaching according to individual talent", "learning
and re-learning", and "learning about new things by re-
viewing old things". He, in fact, stressed the importance
of strengthening whatever knowledge one had already
had. As for the attitude towards the learning process, he
advocated honesty and candidness. "When you know,
say you know," he advised. "When you do not know, say
you do not know." His words and deeds were compiled
by his students to form a book entitled *The Analects of
Confucius*. Confucius was reported to have edited *Book
of Odes*, *Book of History*, *Book of Change*, *Spring and
Autumn Annals*, and some other works. Later, they were
referred to as the Confucian Classics.

3. BEGINNING OF FEUDAL SOCIETY:
WARRING STATES PERIOD (475-221 B.C.)

The feudal society of China began during the Warring States Period. It ended in the middle decades of the
19th century when the British capitalist class launched
aggression against China that precipitated the Opium
War. It had a history of more than 2,300 years.

**Establishment of Feudalism During the Warring
States Period.** The newly emerged landlord class took
over power in the various states and established the feudal
system towards the end of the Spring and Autumn Period.
After many years of ferocious warfare aimed at expansion
and annexation, only seven states survived by the Warring States Period. The seven states, that checked and
balanced one another, were Qi, Chu, Yan, Han, Zhao,
Wei, and Qin. To cope with the new situation, each of the
states initiated reforms, at one time or another. The
earliest reform was carried out in Wei by Li Kui, but the
most thorough of the reforms took place in Qin. Accept-
ing the proposals of Shang Yang, the Qin government
abolished the well-field system and legally recognized
private ownership of land which could be bought or sold.
It promoted tilling and weaving so as to increase the production of essentials; it abolished privileges enjoyed by
hereditary aristocrats; it granted land and titles to those
who had distinguished themselves on the battlefield. All
officials must be appointed by the central government,
and a feudal dictatorship was thus established. As a result of carrying out the kind of reforms as outlined above,
the Qin state became rich and strong. The establishment
of feudalism, meanwhile, had sped up the development
of culture as well as the economy. Instruments made of

iron and ploughing by oxen became popular over a wider and wider area. Ximen Bao of Wei, channelling the water of the Zhanghe River for irrigation, helped agricultural production in his state. The Dujiang Dam in Sichuan and the Zhengguo Canal in Guanzhong were among the largest irrigation projects constructed by Qin. Meanwhile, agriculture and handicraft industry progressed noticeably, and commerce and cities became more and more prosperous. Linzi in Qi, Handan in Zhao, Luoyang in Zhou, Ying in Chu, Ji in Yan, and Xianyang in Qin — they were all famous cities during the Warring States Period. In Linzi, capital of Qi, there were royal palaces, markets, and busy streets crowded with vehicles, horses, and pedestrians. The city had a circumference of more than 20 kilometres; it contained, among other things, six iron-smelting factories, and also factories making copper and bone articles. Money had been introduced to facilitate exchange, and each of the states had its own currency.

A Hundred Schools Contended. During the Warring States Period, many schools of philosophy flourished, such as Mohism, Confucianism, Legalism, and Taoism. Each school presented its own writings, propagating its own beliefs while criticizing the beliefs of others. Together they created a situation in which "a hundred schools contended".

Mohism was a school of philosophy pioneered by Mo Zi (c. 478-392 B.C.) whose real name was Mo Di. A native of Lu (some historians say Song), he at one time worked as an artisan. He advocated "universal love", "pacifism", and "honouring of the virtuous", all of which reflected the wish of small producers at that time. He had many followers and exercised great influence on the society of his time. The book *Mo Zi* represented the collective works of Mohist philosophers.

The representative works of Taoism are *Lao Zi* and *Zhuang Zi*. The former is also known as *Book of Taoist Virtue*, attributed to a man by the name of Lao Dan, a historian-official of the Zhou Dynasty. Actually it was written by an anonymous author of the Warring States Period. Facing great changes in contemporary society, the author injected uncertainty into things with which man was most concerned, such as honour and disgrace, fortune and misfortune, strength and weakness. From the concept of uncertainty and changeability, he developed elementary dialectics. He believed that there was nothing man could do regarding the change of events which was controlled by the "way of heaven". What man could and ought to do was to follow nature, remaining passive and "doing nothing in particular". His ideal society was one "small in size and sparse in population", where people had neither desire nor knowledge and "do not communicate with one another for the entire duration of their lives". *Zhuang Zi* was written by Zhuang Zhou (c. 369-286 B.C.) and his students. He was even more pessimistic than the author of *Lao Zi*.

Mencius (c. 372-289 B.C.) was a principal representative of Confucianism during the Warring States Period. His real name was Meng Ke, and he hailed from the state of Zou (in modern Zouxian, Shandong Province). A student of Confucius' grandson Zi Si, he considered himself the master's ideological descendant. He advocated "the kingly way" and "the policy of benevolence", advising all the rulers to win the hearts of their subjects so as to secure their own rule. He had numerous disciples and travelled from state to state. As for his words and thought, they were recorded in *Meng Zi*, a work compiled by his students.

Xun Zi (c. 313-238 B.C.), whose real name was Xun Kuang or Xun Qing, was a native of Zhao. His ideas were recorded in a book entitled *Xun Zi*. Though considered a member of the Confucian school, he criticized, as well as absorbed and developed, the thought of Confucius and Mencius. Needless to say, he also criticized and absorbed other schools of philosophy. He believed that man could conquer nature, proposing "the utilization of all that heaven offers for the benefit of man". A student must be superior to his teacher eventually, he said, just as "green, that is derived from blue, is superior to blue". His philosophy contains some elements of materialism.

Han Fei (c. 280-233 B.C.), a student of Xun Zi's, was a native of Han. His ideas could be found in a book entitled *Han Fei Zi*. He opposed such concepts as heavenly mandate and questioned the existence of ghosts and spirits. He had no use for "returning to the old" and opposed retrogression as a matter of principle. He advocated the concentration of all power in the hands of the sovereign, and rule by law. He was a representative of the Legalist school. After the unification of China by the Qin state, much of his advocacy was put into practice and further developed.

As for the school of military science, its principal representatives were Sun Wu of the Spring and Autumn Period and Sun Bin of the Warring States Period. The former wrote *Military Science of Sun Zi* and the latter *Military Science of Sun Bin*. Both expressed thought on military strategy and tactics that contained in them elements of dialectics.

As for literature, the poetry written by Qu Yuan (340-278 B.C.) stood above all others. The poet was a native of Chu and had been exiled by his government more than once. He wrote *Li Sao* (*The Lament*) and many other poems. By adopting the style of popular songs, he created a new style known as "Chu songs". The new style exercised great influence on poetry writing of later ages.

4. GROWTH OF FEUDAL SOCIETY: QIN AND HAN TIMES (221 B.C.-A.D. 220)

Qin (221-207 B.C.), China's First Feudal Dynasty. During the Warring States Period, the movement towards unification was made possible through wars of annexation. For the first part of this period, partial unification was achieved when large states, by means of war, absorbed their small neighbours. The second part of this period was marked by wars of annexation among the "Powerful Seven" themselves. Upon his ascension to the throne, Ying Zheng (r. 246-210 B.C.), King of Qin, embarked upon a career of conquest. Preparing well, he successively annexed and terminated Han, Zhao, Wei, Chu, Yan, and Qi. In 221 B.C., his effort was crowned with success when China was unified under Qin.

The unification of China was followed by the establishment of a highly centralized feudal regime, the first of its kind in Chinese history. To elevate his own position, Ying Zheng awarded himself a new title "Huangdi". The new title, based upon the reading of legends, has been translated as "emperor". He called himself "First Emperor", to be followed, said he, by

"Second Emperor", "Third Emperor", etc. "until eternity to come".

Having concentrated all power in his own hands, the First Emperor of Qin proceeded with the establishment of a huge bureaucracy headed by himself. Under him were two premiers (left and right) responsible for administration, one grand chancellor responsible for military affairs, and one grand consor responsible for supervision of government officials as well as the management of governmental records. The three highest officials — premier(s), grand chancellor, and grand censor — were jointly referred to as "Three Dukes". Under the "Three Dukes" were "Nine Secretaries of State" in charge of the various departments in the central government. All important officials in the central government were appointed by the emperor who could transfer or dismiss them as he chose.

For the empire as a whole, the First Emperor adopted a system of prefectures and counties whereby the nation was divided first into 36 and later into 40 prefectures. In each prefecture there were governor in charge of administration, prefectural chancellor in charge of military affairs, and prefectural censor in charge of the supervision of officials. Under each prefecture were counties, each of which was headed by a magistrate in charge of administration. Below the administrative level of counties were townships headed by "three elders" and wards headed by chiefs. The heads of prefectures and counties were appointed by and responsible to the emperor. They must obey and carry out the emperor's orders without reservation, so that the law and the policy as determined by him would be uniformly enforced throughout the nation.

The system of central dictatorship, as adopted by the First Emperor of the Qin Dynasty, had the greatest impact on the feudal society of China for more than 2,000 years. Every subsequent dynasty followed the Qin example without basic changes.

As a result of the long-time division of China, each state had its own script of writing during the Warring States Period. Upon its unification of China, the Qin government promoted the Small Script, a simplier form that had, comparatively speaking, fewer strokes for Chinese characters, as the standard for official writing across China. Later, another script, known as *li*, was also used. The *li* script, in fact, was similar to the *kai* script that has been in vogue through the centuries. Besides the written script, the Qin government also standardized currencies as well as weights and measures. To facilitate transportation, it not only ordered the removal or destruction of all the check-posts, fortifications, and castles, set up or built by the six states prior to the unification; but it also constructed "express highways" that radiated from Xianyang, the capital, towards the northeast, north China, and the southeast. Each of the "express highways" measured 50 paces in width, shouldered by trees. All these measures, as described above, strengthened the country's unity under a feudal regime.

To strengthen his own rule, the First Emperor ordered the burning of books other than those approved by the Qin government, and the burying alive of dissident scholars. He also ordered the destruction of all military weapons that had been scattered among the populace.

To prevent the Xiongnu (Hun) aristocracy from marching southward to invade China, the First Emperor ordered General Meng Tian to mobilize huge manpower

to link all the walls that had been built, for the purpose
of defence against the Xiongnu, by the states of Qin, Zhao,
Yan, and others before the unification. The result was
the Great Wall that began in the west at Lintao (to the
north of modern Minxian, Gansu Province) and ended in
the east at Liaodong (to the north of modern Liaoyang,
Liaoning Province). It stretched for thousands of
kilometres

Peasant Uprisings Towards the End of Qin. Corvee
and taxation were most onerous during the Qin Dynasty.
Regular taxes alone constituted two-thirds of a peasant's
harvest. Besides, the peasant must perform duties as a
soldier and do unpaid labour. The total number of
peasants recruited to build the Epang Palace, the Lishan
Mausoleum, and the Great Wall, and of those recruited
as soldiers for the defence of the frontier exceeded two
million. The brutal oppression and the ruthless exploitation gave the peasants no choice but to resist. In the
seventh lunar month of 209 B.C., Chen Sheng and Wu
Guang, together with 900 other peasants, were drafted
and sent to Yuyang (modern Miyun, Beijing) to perform
military duties. When they arrived at Daze Township of
Qixian (to the southwest of modern Suxian, Anhui Province), there was a sudden downpour, and they could not
arrive in time. Since, according to the Qin law, late arrival
for military duties was punishable by death, they decided
that they might as well start a rebellion. They staged an
armed uprising at Daze and quickly occupied Chenxian
(modern Huaiyang, Henan Province). They announced
the establishment of a new regime called Zhangchu, of
which Chen Sheng was the king and Wu Guang the
military commander. They called upon all the people in
China to revolt against the Qin regime. It was this kind

of violence, spearheaded by peasants who had nothing as
weapons other than hoes and clubs, that eventually toppl-
ed the Qin Dynasty.

Establishment and Consolidation of Western Han.
After the death of Chen Sheng and Wu Guang, Liu Bang
(256–195 B.C.), one of the peasant leaders, eventually
unified the country and established the Han regime. The
capital of the new regime was Changan (northwest of
modern Xi'an, Shaanxi Province), and the regime has been
referred to by historians as Western Han (206 B.C.-A.D.
24). Liu Bang is also known by his imperial appellation
Emperor Gaozu of Han. As for governmental structure,
the new regime followed the example of its predecessor
Qin by adopting the system of "Three Dukes and Nine
Secretaries of State" for the central government and the
system of prefectures and counties for the country as a
whole. Even its laws were similar to those of the Qin
regime. It awarded many with the titles of dukes or
princes, who received fiefs for support. In due course,
these dukedoms and principalities became powerful and
strong; they were virtually independent kingdoms. In
154 B.C., seven of them openly revolted; upon the
collapse of the revolt, all the areas they formerly controlled were brought under central administration. During the reign of Emperor Wudi (r. 141–87 B.C.), more
than 100 hereditary domains were abolished, and the
country was then divided into 13 provinces, each of which
was headed by a governor appointed by the central
government. The governor, in turn, supervised the work
of district magistrates under his jurisdiction. Salt making, iron smelting, and coinage were declared governmental monopolies, and the concentration of power in
the hands of the central government was further

strengthened. Meanwhile, the relationship between different nationalities in China became closer and closer. One might say that China under the Western Han was a united and strong feudal state having many nationalities.

Social economy progressed during the Western Han period. As a result of the peasant war towards the end of the Qin Dynasty, many peasants succeeded in regaining a large portion of land and properties they had lost, and many slaves were emancipated. An opportune situation for production came about, as living conditions for the people had improved. The incentive for production was high, and social economy advanced as a result. Having witnessed the power of peasants during the period of peasant war and having learned a lesson from the quick collapse of the Qin regime, the rulers of Western Han, to strengthen their governance as well as to increase governmental revenue, paid particular attention to the promotion of agriculture and handicrafts. They carried out a policy of "less corvée and light taxation", so as to "enable the nation to recuperate and build up its strength". Needless to say, a policy of this kind was most beneficial to economic recovery and development.

The advance made in agriculture and the popular use of iron implements in farming can be inferred from the recent discovery of such implements dating back to the Western Han period, in the provinces of Liaoning, Gansu, Hunan, and Sichuan, and also areas further beyond. In fact, innovations were continually made in the manufacturing of iron tools for farming. During the reign of Emperor Wudi, Zhao Guo, then in charge of army provisions, invented a kind of plough drawn by two oxen harnessed together, a drill barrow and other farming tools. Zhao Guo, as an expert on farming, also introduced the system in which a furrow and its ridges would take turns to lie idle, so that soil fertility would be restored after one year's rest. Large numbers of irrigation works were constructed and extensive areas of wasteland reclaimed. As a result, agriculture progressed on an unprecedented scale, and the production of grain crops increased by a sizable amount. *The Book of Fan Shengzhi*, a definitive work on farming that appeared during this period, reflected the advanced level of agricultural technology that had been attained thus far.

Meanwhile, the handicraft industry also made progress. The iron industry, responsible for the manufacturing of large quantities of farming implements, hand tools, utensils, and weapons, was operated on a huge scale. Not only the quantity of iron products increased, but their quality improved as well. The salt industry, meanwhile, made a steady progress of its own. As for the technology of manufacturing silk, the people of Western Han had new accomplishments in spinning, weaving, and dyeing. They now knew how to make brocade. Inside a Han tomb unearthed at Mawangdui, Changsha, there were more than 100 items of silk dating back to the early period of Western Han. Each of these items was elegant, beautiful, and well-made. Particularly impressive was a jacket made of thin silk that weighed less than one ounce. The craftsmanship was excellent. Then the cities of Linzi and Chengdu were two major centres of the textile industry.

Co-operation Among Nationalities Strengthened. Early during the Western Han Dynasty, the Xiongnu were most active on the vast expanse of nothern China. Frequently they traded with the Han people, exchanging horses and animal skins for agricultural and handicraft products. However, frictions of a military nature often occurred between the slave-owning Xiongnu aristocracy and the royal house of the Han. In 127 B.C., 121 B.C., and again in 119 B.C., Emperor Wudi dispatched generals like Wei Qing and Huo Qubing, at the head of large concentrations of troops, for the defeat of the Xiongnu. Later, Huhanye, chief of the Xiongnu, expressed friendship for the Western Han, and the latter, then headed by Emperor Yuandi, married princess Wang Zhaojun to him. After the marriage, envoys from each visited the other often, and the relationship between the two peoples became closer and closer.

During the period of the Western Han, the minority nationalities who lived in China's northeast included the Yilou, the Fuyu, the Xianbei, and the Wuyuan. The minority nationalities who lived in today's Zhejiang, Fujian, Guangdong, and Guangxi were known collectively as the Baiyue, while those in today's Yunnan and Guizhou were collectively referred to as the Southwestern Yi. The minority nationalities in China's northwest included, principally, the Di and the Qiang. All these nationalities maintained long-time, close relations with people in the interior regions. They and the Han people worked together, diligently, in developing the frontier regions of the motherland.

The areas to the south and east of Lake Balkhash and today's Xinjiang were known in ancient times as the Western Regions. In 138 B.C. and again in 119 B.C., Emperor Wudi dispatched Zhang Qian, at the head of a delegation including Gan Fu, to visit these regions as a special envoy. The trips were instrumental in promoting the economic and cultural relations between the Han people and the nationalities there. From then on, the government of Western Han frequently sent envoys to the

Western Regions, and the latter, in return, also sent representatives to Changan. The planting of grapes, garlics, walnuts, and sesames was imported from there; so were certain music and dances. The people of these regions, in turn, learned from the Han the technology of smelting iron, digging wells, and farming. In 60 B.C. (second year of Shenjue, reign of Emperor Xuandi), the Western Han regime established at Bugur (near modern Luntai, Xinjiang) the Western Regions Administration that had jurisdiction over a vast expanse covering the areas north of the Kunlun Mountains and those on both sides of the Tianshan Mountains and extending westward to as far as Lake Balkhash.

Social Crisis of Western Han and Wang Mang's Reform. During the later period of the Western Han, aristocrats, high officials, and big landlords competed with one another in seizing more and more land for themselves. As they took over much of the rich farmland, the peasants were left with very little. The landless either became homeless refugees or sold themselves as slaves. As social contradiction deepened, peasant uprisings became more frequent. The Western Han regime itself was endangered as a result. In 6 A.D., Wang Mang, a relative of the royal house, usurped power and replaced Emperor Pingdi as sovereign. In 9 A.D., he formally announced the establishment of a new dynasty named Xin. To ease the social contradiction, he proceeded to conduct reforms in many spheres including the bureaucracy, currency, land system, taxation, and governmental monopolies. But these reforms bore little relevance to reality. Besides, they were too complex, and the laws governing them changed often. All this merely increased the people's sense of insecurity and the instabil-

ity of society as a whole. As social crisis was built up to
a climax, peasant uprisings of major proportions erupted.

Uprisings of Green Woodsmen and Red Eyebrows.
The army of the Green Woodsmen was created in the
Green Woods Mountains, Dangyang County, Hubei Province. Its leaders were Wang Kuang and Wang Feng. In
17 A.D., they raised the standard of revolt, to which the
nearby peasants responded with enthusiasm. Later, they
left the Green Woods Mountains and fought in Nanjun
(modern Jiangling, Hubei Province), Nanyang (modern
Nanyang, Henan Province), and other places. In a ferocious battle fought at Kunyang (modern Yexian, Henan
Province), they destroyed Wang Mang's main forces. They
entered Changan in triumph, as they successfully ended
Wang Mang's regime.

In 18 A.D., Fan Chong, the principal leader of another
rebel group, the Red Eyebrows, led peasants to stage an
armed uprising in Juxian, Shandong Province. Using Mt.
Taishan as the base of their operation, he and his followers fought in Shandong and also in the northern section of Jiangsu. Very quickly, they developed into an
insurgent army of more than a hundred thousand men.
To distinguish themselves from their enemy, they painted
their eyebrows red before they went to battle. That was
why they were referred to as the Red Eyebrows.

Simultaneously with but independent of the Green
Woodsmen and the Red Eyebrows were tens of other insurgent units that fought against the government on the
vast plain north of the Huanghe River, including today's
Hebei and Shandong provinces.

Politics and Economics of Eastern Han. In 25 A.D.,
Liu Xiu (5 B.C.-A.D. 57), a powerful landlord who had
wormed his way into the ranks of the peasant insurgents

declared himself emperor and re-established the Han regime. Since the capital of the re-established regime, Luoyang, was located to the east of Changan, historians refer to the new regime as the Eastern Han (25-220 A.D.). Known also as Emperor Guangwu, Liu Xiu brutally crushed the peasant insurgents.

Roughly speaking, the Eastern Han regime followed the example of its predecessor the Western Han regime in terms of political institutions. Six times, Emperor Guangwu decreed the emancipation of slaves, and many slaves gained their freedom as a result. Later, he distributed some of the government-owned land among poverty-stricken peasants whom he also lent seeds, farm implements, and food grain. He paid particular attention to the construction of irrigation works, the control of the Huanghe River and the building of embankments along its course. The efforts paid off handsomely, as the Huanghe River did not change its course in the next 800 years. The technology of smelting iron improved further during the Eastern Han Dynasty. Du Shi, magistrate of Nanyang, invented a device that used running water to push wheels which in turn operated on bellow-like baggings of animal skins to generate continuous wind for the furnace. In this way, the temperature inside the furnace would be increased, and the quality of the finished iron improved. Meanwhile, improvement was made in the production of well salt.

The Eastern Han regime came about as a result of the support given to it by powerful landlords who, therefore, enjoyed special privileges. They robbed small farmers of their land and built large plantations that were economically self-sufficient. They were a power to be reckoned with in local politics, and militarily they had under their control a number of "family soldiers". They tended to assert independence in relation to the central authorities. Some of them worked as local officials, while others held power in the central government. During the latter part of the Eastern Han period, eunuchs and empresses' relatives took turns in the enjoyment of supreme power; they openly traded in official ranks and extorted money from the people. Many peasants, having lost their land and other means of subsistence, drifted into refugees. There were peasant uprisings as early as 107. For the next 70 to 80 years, more than 100 peasant uprisings broke out in the country.

Yellow-Turban Rebellion. In 184, the Yellow Turbans' rebellion exploded on a nationwide scale. Its principal leader was a man named Zhang Jiao, a native of Julu (located to the south of modern Ningjin, Hebei Province). Originally the leader of a Taoist sect named Doctrine of Peace, he became well-known as a physician and a proselytizer. Successful in propaganda and in organization for a long period, he had as followers as many as several hundred thousand impoverished peasants, who were politically active in the valleys of the Huanghe and Changjiang rivers. In the second lunar month of 184, the standard of revolt was raised. As the rebels wrapped their heads with yellow turbans so as to distinguish themselves from their enemy, they were called Yellow Turbans. They fought many battles and won many victories; at one time, they surrounded Luoyang, capital of the Eastern Han, on all sides. However, pressured by an alliance between the regular army and the militias organized by landlords, they, after a heroic struggle that lasted nine months, finally met with defeat. Nevertheless, even after the main force had been destroyed, the rem-

nants continued the struggle for more than 20 years.
The revolt launched by the Yellow Turbans marked the
first well-prepared, well-organized peasant uprising in the
history of China. They delivered a severe blow to the rich
landlords who had grabbed more and more land. The
rebellion contributed materially to the disintegration of
the Eastern Han regime.

Culture During the Qin-Han Period. Culture bloom-
ed during the Qin-Han period. In writing *Records of the
Historian*, Sima Qian (c. 145-90 B.C.) pioneered the use
of biographies in the writing of a general history. Ban
Gu (32-92 A.D.), who wrote *History of the Han Dynasty*,
was the first dynastic historian. The methods introduced
by these two authors proved to be, for the next 2,000
years, the model for other historians who wished to write
"official histories". As for literature, there were *fu* written by Sima Xiangru (180-118 B.C.) and Jia Yi (200-168
B.C.). *Fu*, incidentally, was a lengthy form of poetry
developed from the "Chu songs". In the field of
philosophy, the materialist Wang Chong (27-c. 97 A.D.)
wrote *Discourses Weighed in the Balance*, in which he
boldly refuted superstitions then favoured by the government. In fine arts, the Han Dynasty was most noted for
its achievement in stone and brick carvings. Its drawings
on grave bricks and lacquer products also constituted
a major contribution in the history of Chinese art. In
science, there was a famous work entitled *Nine Chapters
of the Mathematical Art* that introduced many new concepts that were very advanced for their time, such as the
four basic operations of fractions, the operations of posi-
tive and negative numbers, and the concept of decimal
fractions. Zhang Heng invented an armillary sphere
powered by running water; it automatically and correctly

projected the movement of heavenly bodies. He also invented a seismograph that showed the direction of earthquakes and an instrument to detect the direction of wind. Cai Lun, synthesizing the experience of the labouring masses, improved the skill of making paper, as he, for the first time in the history of China, used tree bark, odds and ends of hemp, cloth rags, and discarded fishing nets as raw materials. Needless to say, the invention of paper was a great contribution to the development and exchange of world cultures. As for medicine, Zhang Zhongjing wrote *On Typhoid Fevers and Other Diseases* that had a great impact on ancient medicine. He was then hailed as a medical saint. Contemporary with him was another medical talent by the name of Hua Tuo who was as versatile as he was particularly proficient in acupuncture and surgery. He was the first in the world to use anaesthetics during surgery.

Cultural and Economic Exchange with Foreign Countries. The cultural and economic exchange between China and foreign countries made substantial progress during the Qin-Han period. As early as the reign of Emperor Wudi, contacts were made with the island country of Japan. In 57 A.D., a Japanese kingdom named Yamato dispatched an envoy bearing gifts to China. Emperor Guangwu of the Eastern Han presented the king of this kingdom with a golden seal. In 1784, the seal was discovered in Kyushu of Japan. During the Qin-Han period, Chinese products made of copper, iron, and silks were shipped to Japan from time to time, while weapons and other Japanese products also came to China.

China made contact with many countries in Southeast and South Asia during the Western Han period. By the sea routes, one could then start at modern Xuwen County,

Guangdong Province, or modern Hepu County, Guangxi
Zhuang Autonomous Region, and sail amid the islands in
the South China Sea until one reached countries on
the Malay Peninsula and along the Burmese coast, or the
kingdom of Kanci in India. Contacts were also established
between China and a number of countries in West Asia
through land routes in the Western Regions. When
Zhang Qian went to the Western Regions as a special
envoy, he passed through Da Yue Zhi (Indoscythe), located
in today's Pakistan and the northern section of today's
Afghanistan. His deputy went to Sindhu, located in
today's Nepal and India, and Kasmira which was part of
today's Kashmir. Then Buddhism, that originated in Nepal
and India, had already arrived in the Western Regions,
from which it gradually spread to China's hinterland. At
this time Chinese cloth, made in Sichuan, could be found
in India. On their way to the Western Regions, Zhang
Qian and his deputy passed through Bactria, located in
the northern section of modern Afghanistan, Parthia that
was in today's Iran and Iraq, and other countries. From
then on, China and these countries frequently exchanged
envoys, and merchants of both sides also visited each
other. It was during this time that the Chinese technology
of smelting iron and digging well was transported to these
countries. Chinese silk and iron and steel were most
popular, and some of them were transshipped to Rome.
Meanwhile, the agricultural and art products of West
Asia were transported to China. After Zhang Qian's
journeys to the Western Regions, the various countries
there sent envoys to Changan on a regular basis. In one
case, a special envoy to Changan was accompanied by a
Roman magician who could perform such high-level
tricks as "swallowing swords and spitting fire".

Beginning at Changan, capital of Western Han, a trade route passed through the Gansu Corridor, the oases to the north and south of the Tarim Basin, the Pamirs and Central and West Asia, finally reaching ports along the eastern coast of the Mediterranean. This route stretched for a distance of more than 7,000 kilometres. It was the longest and the most important trade route by land in the ancient world. Since it was most noted for transporting silk from China, it was referred to as the Silk Road. Over mountains and deserts, envoys and merchants, horses and camel caravans — all of them had travelled on this long, seemingly endless road. Needless to say, people of all countries along this route made great contribution to the friendship and understanding between nations, not to mention their constructive role in facilitating international trade.

5. GRAND UNION OF NATIONALITIES AND ECONOMIC DEVELOPMENT: THREE KINGDOMS, TWO JINS, AND SOUTHERN AND NORTHERN DYNASTIES (220-589)

Three Legs of a Tripod: Wei, Shu, and Wu. The storm started by the Yellow Turbans ended the Eastern Han regime all but in name. In the process of trying to suppress them, local officials and powerful landlords recruited or expanded armies of their own, and quickly they developed into territorial magnates, over whom the central government had no control. They fought among themselves in order to gain territories at each other's expense. Finally, Cao Cao (155-220) gained control over the Huanghe River valley, Liu Bei (161-223) the province

of Sichuan, and Sun Quan (182-252) the middle and lower
Changjiang valley. The kingdoms they established were
known, respectively, as Wei (220-265), with capital at
Luoyang, Shu (221-263), with capital at Chengdu, and Wu
(229-280), with capital at Nanjing. The three kingdoms,
like three legs of a tripod, coexisted until 280 when the
Western Jin unified the country.

Because of the incessant warfare towards the end
of the Eastern Han and throughout the period of the Three
Kingdoms, the assurance of food supply for the military
was an important problem for all leaders to face. Cao
Cao, an outstanding statesman of the landlord class,
established military fields along the Huanghe River, and
repaired and constructed irrigation works to nourish
them. As a result, agricultural production in north China
recovered quickly and then progressed. The Kingdom
of Shu, whose leader had the advice of Zhuge Liang
(181-234), another outstanding statesman and military
strategist, paid particular attention to agricultural production. It efficiently maintained the irrigation works
centred on the Dujiang Dam, and encouraged and promoted economic development among the minority
nationalities in southern Sichuan and Yunnan and Guizhou provinces. The Kingdom of Wu promoted not only
agricultural production but also the shipbuilding industry
and the maritime trade. Some of the ships it built were
more than 200 feet in length. As early as the Eastern Han
period, the people in Yizhou (modern Taiwan) conducted
trade along China's southeastern coast. In 230, the Kingdom of Wu dispatched Wei Wen and Zhuge Zhi, at the
head of a fleet with 10,000 men, which sailed towards
Yizhou. The undertaking helped the establishment of a

close relationship between the people in Taiwan and the people on the mainland.

Western Jin: Brief Period of Unification. Of the Three Kingdoms, Wei was the strongest. In 263, it conquered Shu. In 265, Sima Yan (236-290), its powerful minister, replaced the Wei regime with a new regime of his own, namely, Jin. Historians refer to this new regime as Western Jin (265-316). In 280, the Sima family conquered Wu, ending the tripartite relationship and briefly unifying China.

The government of Western Jin was corrupt, as it selected officials not on merit but on the background of the candidates' families. As a result, the government was controlled by a hereditary elite. An official, as a member of the elite, enjoyed the special privilege of owning not only large tracts of land but also peasants whose status was similar to that of a serf. He, as a member of the ruling class, lived a life of luxury and corruption. To strengthen its control of the country, the royal house elevated many of its members to the position of dukes or kings, but the scramble for power soon led to the "Rioting of the Eight Kings" that lasted 16 years. The internecine warfare between these kings brought nothing but utter disaster to the people. The regime was considerably weakened as a result.

Beginning with the Eastern Han period, the minority nationalities who lived along China's northern and western frontiers moved south of the Great Wall one after another, where they cohabited with the Han people. As the burden on peasants became more and more unbearable during the Western Jin period and as natural disasters and pestilence raged on from year to year, the peasants, who could no longer find a livelihood at home, left for the outside world to seek a subsistence to keep themselves alive. Liu Yuan, a member of the Xiongnu aristocracy who cohabited with the Han, took advantage of the peasants' grievances against the Western Jin government and raised the standard of revolt. He attacked and captured Luoyang and Changan and thus ended the Western Jin regime.

Eastern Jin and the Sixteen Northern States. In 317, the year after the Western Jin was terminated, Sima Rui, King of Langya, established a new regime in the south, with its capital at Jiankang (modern Nanjing, Jiangsu Province). The new regime, which lasted more than 100 years (317-420), is referred to by historians as the Eastern Jin.

While the Eastern Jin maintained its rule in the south, north China entered an era of long political division. Aristocrats of some of the minority nationalities and powerful Han landlords created more than 20 local regimes in the Huanghe River valley and in Sichuan during this period. Of them, only 16 were of considerable duration or strength, and they are referred to by historians as "the Sixteen States". They kept on fighting among themselves in total confusion.

One of these states was the Former Qin (351-394) which, under the leadership of Fu Jian, became strong as a result of conducting much-needed reforms. It temporarily unified north China towards the end of the fourth century. In 383, Fu Jian, at the head of several hundred thousand men, invade the Eastern Jin. The latter dispatched Xie Xuan and Xie Shi to command an army for the purpose of defence. The two sides met across Feishui River (south of modern Shouxian, Anhui Province), and Xie Xuan, taking advantage of the invader's arrogance

and complacence, decisively defeated him. Fu Jian fled
north in a hurry after his defeat in the historically famous
encounter, known as the Battle of the Feishui River.

Southern and Northern Dynasties. The battle that
the Eastern Jin won at the Battle of the Feishui River
spared south China from war devastation; it enabled that
region to continue its economic and cultural development.
In 420, General Liu Yu ended the Eastern Jin regime and
established a regime of his own, known as Song (420-470).
For the next 160 years, south China was ruled, successively, by four regimes: Song, Qi (479-502), Liang (502-
557), and Chen (557-589). Their capital was Jiankang.
Historians refer to them as Southern Dynasties.

The Former Qin regime soon collapsed after the
Battle of the Feishui River, and many feuding, local regimes took its place. With the progress of time, the
aristocratic clan of Tuoba, a member of the Xianbei tribe,
gradually unified north China and, in 386, established a
new regime in the western section of modern Inner
Mongolia and the northern section of modern Shanxi.
The official title of the new regime was Wei, with its
capital at Pingcheng (modern Datong, Shanxi Province),
but historians refer to it as Northern Wei (386-534). Later,
Northern Wei was split into Eastern Wei (534-550) and
Western Wei (535-557), and then into Northern Qi (550-
577) and Northern Zhou (557-581). These five regimes
have been referred to as Northern Dynasties.

The Southern and Northern Dynasties were in fact
a continuation of the political division dating back to the
Eastern Jin period.

Social and Economic Development. During the
Southern Dynasties, south China made great progress in
economic development. In agriculture, the peasants, by

taking advantage of the favourable conditions of abun-
dant water supply and clement weather, brought about
two harvests of paddy rice per year. As agricultural production increased, the areas south of the Changjiang
River became an important granary for the nation as a
whole. The handicraft industry, meanwhile, also made
speedy progress. The technology of spinning and weaving
had been so improved that in areas like Yuzhang (modern
Nanchang, Jiangxi Province) yarns washed in the late
afternoon could be converted into cloth early the next
morning. The product was called "cloth of rooster's crow"
because it was woven early in the morning when roosters
began to cry aloud. Progress in various degrees was also
made in the manufacturing of paper, salt, lacquerware,
and porcelain, and in the building of ships. Commerce
and cities prospered likewise, and Jiankang developed
into a major commercial centre in south China. As for
foreign trade, Panyu (modern Guangzhou) became a centre of trade with countries of Southeast Asia. The labouring masses in south China contributed greatly to this
development, as they made south China the equal of the
north in terms of economic achievement.

The unification of all areas in the Huanghe River
valley under the Northern Wei strengthened the relationship of all nationalities that had moved there, thus increasing the union of all peoples concerned. Tuoba Hong,
or Emperor Xiaowen (r. 471-499) of the Northern Wei,
carried out a series of reforms, having been benignly influenced by the political experience of the Han landlords.
In 485, he adopted a policy of land equalization, whereby
government-owned land was distributed among house-
holds in accordance with their membership and the
amount of labour power available. The peasants, in

return, must pay the government grain as rent and silk or cloth as tribute, in addition to the performance of labour and military service. Land equalization enabled landless peasants to cultivate abandoned fields, thus laying the foundation of economic recovery for north China, besides increasing governmental revenue and the source of corvée. In 494, Northern Wei moved its capital from Pingcheng to Luoyang, thus strengthening its control over the Central Plains. Meanwhile, the emperor carried out a programme of learning from the Han people by ordering members of the Xianbei nobility to adopt their surnames, wear their costume, speak their language, and intermarry with them. Even his political system was patterned after their model. All these measures made the Northern Wei regime very popular with the Han landlords who thus supported it. Objectively, they sped up the feudalization of Xianbei society and helped the union of all nationalities in north China.

Social contradictions intensified towards the end of the Northern Wei, and the intensification led to a major uprising against the regime waged by the various nationalities north of the Huanghe River. After the collapse of the uprising, the rulers themselves, to attain absolute power, committed fratricide against one another. In the end, the Northern Wei regime itself was split. In 577, the Northern Zhou unified all of north China. Having increased its economic and military strength through the implementation of reform measures, it was in a position to exterminate Chen, its contemporary rival in south China, and unify the whole country.

Cultural Activities During the Three Kingdoms, the Two Jins, and the Southern and Northern Dynasties.

During this period, all cultural activities, including scientific activities, made new progress. Zu Chongzhi (429-500), an outstanding scientist, correctly placed the ratio of the circumference of a circle to its diameter between 3.1415926 and 3.1415927. Jia Sixie, summarizing the labouring people's experience in agriculture and animal husbandry, wrote *Essential Skills in Improving People's Livelihood.* Li Daoyuan (465- or 472-527) wrote *Notes on Water Classic,* an important work on ancient geography. Buddhism, very popular then, was patronized by the ruling class. Fan Zhen (450-515), an original thinker, wrote *On the Extinction of the Soul,* which criticized severely all religions.

As for literature, many good works were produced during this period, especially in the field of five-character poems and literary criticism. Cao Cao, Cao Zhi (192-232), and Tao Yuanming (365-427) were the best-known among the poets. Among the best-known works on literary criticism were *Review of Some Articles* (included in *On Rules of Composition*) by Cao Pi, *Literature Elegant* by Liu Xie, and *On Poetry* by Zhong Rong. The most famous calligrapher and painter were Wang Xizhi and Gu Kaizhi, respectively.

In the wake of Buddhist popularity came the vogue of carving Buddhist deities inside natural or man-made caves. Many of these stone statues have been preserved until this day, such as those in Yungang (in Datong, Shanxi Province), Longmen (near Luoyang, Henan Province), and Dunhuang (in Gansu Province). Sculpturing of all the grand Buddhist statues began during the period in discussion. The magnificence in carving and painting indicates an advanced level of technical skill. Artistically speaking, they are priceless treasures highly valued throughout the world.

Economic and Cultural Exchange with Foreign Countries. In the time of the Former Qin, Buddhism began to spread to Korea from China. Emperor Wudi of Liang of the Southern Dynasties, in response to a request by the king of Paikche, dispatched artisans and painters to Korea. He also sent a scholar named Lu Yi to teach the Koreans Confucian classics and the *Four Histories*, namely, *Records of the Historian, History of the Han Dynasty, History of the Later Han Dynasty,* and *History of the Three Kingdoms*. Acupuncture and calendar making were also introduced to Korea at this time. Meanwhile, the Chinese imported from Korea music and musical instruments. An interchange of this kind enriched the life of people on both sides.

Meanwhile, communication between China and Japan also became more frequent. In 238, Emperor Mingdi of the Wei and the queen of Japan exchanged gifts. During the fourth century, the Chinese who migrated to Japan brought with them the technology involving textiles, pottery, silk reeling, tailoring, and cooking. Chinese books like *The Thousand-Character Classic, The Five Classics,* and *The Analects of Confucius* went to Japan at this time.

During the period of the Three Kingdoms, the Kingdom of Wu once dispatched Kang Tai and Zhu Ying to visit the kingdoms on the Indochina Peninsula, such as Campa (located in the middle section of modern Viet Nam) and Funan (modern Kampuchea). After their return to China, Kang Tai wrote *Stories of Foreign Countries,* and Zhu Ying wrote *Precious Things in Funan*. More than once did Funan send its envoys to China. During

the Liang of the Southern Dynasties, a Funan monk by
the name of Sanghapala came to China and translated
many Buddhist scriptures into his own language. It was
at this time that Chinese architecture and Chinese technology of making paper and textiles were exported to
Viet Nam. Many kingdoms on the Indonesian islands
and Malay Peninsula sent their envoys to China bearing
gifts.

In 399, a 65-year-old monk by the name of Fa Xian
departed from Changan for the Western Regions and
what the Chinese called Tianzhu which covered today's
India, Pakistan, and Bangladesh. He stayed there for three
years and learned the local languages, besides Buddhist
scriptures. He visited Buddha's birthplace in Népal, and
stayed in the kingdom of Simhala (today's Sri Lanka) for
two years before returning to China by the sea route.
Returning home after a journey of 14 years, he wrote a
book entitled *A Record of Buddhist Countries* that
described his observations. The book became invaluable
to the understanding of the history, geography, and customs of the countries in Central Asia, South Asia, and
Southeast Asia. An Indian monk by the name of Kum-
arajiva, who was born in Kuqa of Xinjiang, arrived at
Changan during the period of the Later Qin (384-417).
He translated 300 volumes of Buddhist scriptures and
made great contribution to the cultural exchange between India and China. It was during this period that
Indian medicine, art, and phonology were introduced to
China. At the time of the Eastern Jin, the kingdom of
Simhala dispatched an envoy to present Emperor Andi
with a Buddhist statue that was 4.2 feet in height. During
the Southern Dynasties, the royal house of Gupta in

India corresponded with Emperor Wendi of the Song in China.

Throughout the period of the Three Kingdoms, the Two Jins, and the Southern and Northern Dynasties, many countries in Central and West Asia sent envoys to China in goodwill missions. The Sassanian Dynasty of Persia (Iran) kept close communication with the Northern Wei and Western Wei dynasties. After the Liberation (1949), gold coins used by this Persian dynasty between the fourth and the sixth century were found in the old city of Gaochang near modern Turpan of Xinjiang and also in the old tombs of Shanxian (Henan Province) and Yingde (Guangdong Province). During the period of the Three Kingdoms, Daqin (the Roman Empire which was divided into the Western Roman Empire and the Eastern Roman Empire after 395) had a merchant who met with Sun Quan of the Kingdom of Wu. Official envoys were sent to China by Daqin during the period of the Western Jin. In recent years, three gold coins of the Eastern Roman Empire were discovered in an old tomb of the Northern Qi, that was located in Zanhuang County, Hebei Province. The oldest of the three was coined in 437.

6. APEX OF FEUDAL SOCIETY: SUI, TANG, AND FIVE DYNASTIES AND TEN KINGDOMS (581-960)

Sui's Unification of China. In 581, strongman Yang Jian (541-604) of the Northern Zhou forced the reigning emperor Jingdi to abdicate on his behalf and established a new dynasty named Sui (581-618). From then on, Yang Jian was known as Emperor Wendi, and his capital was

Changan. In 589, he conquered the rival regime in the south named Chen, thus effectively ending the political division of China that, beginning in the period of the Eastern Jin, had persisted for more than 200 years. Finally, China was unified.

For the organization of the central government, Emperor Wendi adopted a system of "Three Administrations and Six Ministries". The Three Administrations were the imperial secretariat, the privy council, and the cabinet, the heads of which were all referred to as prime ministers. They constituted the highest administrative organs of the nation. Under the cabinet were the Six Ministries, namely, the Ministries of Personnel, Finance, Rites, Military Affairs, Justice, and Public Works. The origin of the Three Administrations and Six Ministries could be traced back to the "Three Dukes and Nine Secretaries of State" of the Qin-Han period. As for local administration, it had three levels, province, prefecture, and county. Later, it had only two levels, province (or prefecture) and county. As the power of appointment and dismissal of local officials was once again taken over by the Ministry of Personnel, the central government was further strengthened.

During the Sui Dynasty, each province was required to recommend to the central government three outstanding scholars for possible employment with the government each year. In addition, there were written examinations for the selection of *Xiu Cai* ("Flowering Talents"). Later, other categories were added, such as *Ming Jing* ("Expertise in Classics") and *Jin Shi* ("Advanced Scholarship"). The practice marked the beginning of the civil-service examination system in China.

In the field of economics, the Sui followed the exam-

ple of the Northern Wei by adopting the land equalization system. Peasants' obligations in terms of taxes and
corvée were somewhat lighter, and the Sui society, as a
result, was more stable. Social production increased
enormously. The amount of grain, cloth, and silk collected as taxes was extremely large. The national
granaries were filled to capacity.

To exact as much tribute as possible, especially from
areas south of the Changjiang River, Emperor Yangdi, in
605, ordered the construction of the Grand Canal that
would link north China with south China, so that the
grain and the silk produced in the south could be easily
shipped to the north. After completion, the canal, 2,000
kilometres in length, consisted of four individual canals.
They were, from north to south, the Yongji, the Tongji,
the Hangou, and the Jiangnan. From its central point at
Luoyang, the Grand Canal extended to Zhuojun (located
to the southwest of modern Beijing) in the northeast and
Yuhang (modern Hangzhou) in the southeast. It strengthened the links and facilitated the economic and cultural
exchange between the Changjiang and Huanghe valleys.
It was a vital artery of the body national.

**Peasant Uprisings Towards the End of the Sui
Dynasty. Establishment of the Tang Regime.** During
his reign, Emperor Yangdi (r. 605-618) squandered public
treasure in building palaces for his own comfort and
vanity, and he took three pleasure trips south of the
Changjiang River. The amount of wasted manpower
and financial resources was enormous. Three times he
attempted to conquer Korea, and several million peasants
were drafted as soldiers and labourers for his military
campaigns. As a result, people were exhausted and his
exchequer nearly empty; production was virtually de-

stroyed; and the burden to the peasants had become unbearable. Class contradictions sharpened, leading to peasant uprisings. Among the insurgent groups were the Wagang Army led by Zhai Rang and Li Mi who were active in today's Henan Province; the insurgent army led by Dou Jiande who captured many places in today's Hebei Province; and the insurgent army led by Du Fuwei and Fu Gongshi who were active in the southeastern section of China. Together, they dealt a severe blow to the Sui regime.

While the flame of peasant uprisings was burning across the nation, aristocrats, officials, and landlords recruited troops of their own and occupied this or that part of China. They safeguarded and then extended their power and influence, attempting to take away the fruits of victory that rightly belonged to the peasants. In 617, the aristocrat Li Yuan (565-635) and his son Li Shimin (Emperor Taizong of the Tang, r. 627-649) raised the standard of revolt at Taiyuan and quickly occupied Changan, then the Sui capital. In 618, while under siege in Jiangdu, Emperor Yangdi was assassinated by one of his bodyguards, and his death marked the end of the Sui regime. In the same year, Li Yuan assumed the imperial title at Changan and called his new regime Tang (618-907). The Tang regime brutally crushed the peasant insurgents, eliminated regional power and influence, and unified the country.

Feudal Rule Strengthened During Early Tang. To secure the source of tax revenue, the Tang rulers, in 624, adopted a land equalization system and a tripartite tax system. Under the land equalization system, a peasant above the age of 18 would receive from the government

100 mu of land, of which 20 mu, known as "permanent fields", could be bought or sold, or inherited by his children. The other 80 mu must be returned to the government upon his retirement or death. A widow would receive 30 mu; the allotment would be increased to 50 mu if she was head of a household. Women other than widows would not receive any land at all.

According to the tripartite tax system, an adult male must hand in to the government an annual amount of two piculs of grain as rent, 20 feet of silk and three ounces of floss as tribute. In addition, each year he must render labour service for the government for a period of 20 days. He who did not choose to work would have to pay three feet of silk for each day missed.

Basically, the Tang followed the Sui as far as administrative organizations were concerned. There were, of course, some modifications. In local administration, the two-tier system of provinces and counties prevailed, except in border and strategic areas which were administered by garrison commands. The chief executive of each command was responsible for civil as well as military affairs. During the reign of Emperor Taizong, the nation was divided into 10 territories in accordance with terrain; the division was enlarged to 15 at the time of Emperor Xuanzong. Within the territories there were inspectors-general to supervise the work of provincial and county officials.

, During the reign of Emperor Taizong, *The Code of the Tang Dynasty* in 12 volumes was edited and compiled. His successor, Emperor Gaozong, ordered that each article in the code be elaborated and explained, and the result was *Explanatory Notes on "Code of the Tang*

Dynasty" in 30 volumes. Both works occupy an important position in the legal history of China.

The Tang Dynasty developed further the civil-service examination system that had its beginning during the Sui Dynasty. The categories of examination increased to a dozen or more, including *Xiu Cai, Jin Shi, Ming Jing* and *Ming Fa* ("Expertise in Laws"). The most cherished and emphasized, however, was the category of *Jin Shi*. Those who participated in the examination were either graduates from colleges in the nation's capital or students from the provinces and counties who had been recommended by local governments. In the latter case, the students must pass a preliminary examination on the local level before they could participate in the examination at the nation's capital. Once a candidate passed the latter examination, he would be granted an official post to hold by the Ministry of Personnel. This system of choosing officials by examination strengthened the social foundation of the Tang government.

At the time of Emperor Taizong's reign, the government paid particular attention to the lesson to be learned from history, especially the decline and fall of the Sui regime; consequently, it searched for ways and means to strengthen its own feudal regime. Emperor Taizong was a good listener and accessible to advice, and he encouraged his ministers to express different opinions on political problems, so that the best results could be attained when a policy was carried out. He emphasized the importance of recruiting and employing talented men; this was another reason why he succeeded politically. During his reign, the government was comparatively free of abuse, and the nation was strong.

Emperor Taizong was succeeded by his son Li Zhi,

known in history as Emperor Gaozong. During Gaozong's
reign, the power of the state was gradually taken over by
his consort Wu Zetian. In 690, she changed the dynastic
title of Tang to that of Zhou and assumed the imperial
title. Not until 705 when she died was the dynastic title
of Tang restored. During the time of her reign, the
political health of the Tang regime, nurtured by Emperor
Taizong, had not yet deteriorated; social economy continued to make progress.

Economic Prosperity of the Tang Dynasty. The first
half of the Tang Dynasty was characterized by political
unification, social stability, and enthusiasm among the
labourers. All this, in turn, created a favourable environ-
ment for economic progress. In agriculture, the Tang
people invented the ingenious "crooked plough" which
enabled the peasant to control the depth of the soil to
which it went. Needless to say, a plough of this kind
was helpful to the crops' growth. The Tang government
paid attention to the construction of irrigation works; it
was at this time that a type of water wheel with bamboo
or wooden tubes, and another type for bringing water to
higher ground were invented. The development of irrigation facilities helped the transformation of wasteland
into fertile fields, thus increasing agricultural production.
Tea was a cash crop developed during the Tang Dynasty,
and it was planted in many areas of south China. Large
tea plantations also appeared.

The handicraft industry also made good progress
during the Tang Dynasty. Division of labour was minute
in government-owned factories, and the number of
privately-owned factories increased considerably during
this period. It was reported that He Mingyuan, a wealthy
merchant in Dingzhou (Zhengding, modern Hebei Prov-

ince) owned 500 looms. The skill of making handicraft products also improved enormously. The traditional way of spinning and weaving silk became more refined, and there were more than 100 copper, iron, silver, and tin mining and smelting establishments scattered across the country.

The manufacturing of porcelains reached a new level of excellence during this period. The most famous and the best were produced in Xingzhou (Xingtai, modern Hebei Province) and Yuezhou (Shaoxing, modern Zhejiang Province). Tang kilns produced a large quantity of celadon ware that was noted for its high quality, especially its colouring. The celebrated Tang tricolour pottery had indeed three colours — yellow, green, and purple (or blue) — baked into the products during the firing process. The colouring looked bright and fresh, and the products themselves took many shapes and forms. They were world-famous for the beauty they conveyed.

Considerable progress was made in shipbuilding and paper making.

The Tang Dynasty was also noted for its commercial activities, as cities and towns mushroomed across the country. Among the famous cities were Changan, Luoyang, Yangzhou, Jiangzhou (Jiangling, modern Hubei Province), Mingzhou (Ningbo, modern Zhejiang Province), Chengdu, and Bianzhou.

The centre of transportation was Changan, wherefrom radiated all the major highways. Eastward the highway network went as far as the Shandong Peninsula; westward it passed through Qizhou (Fengxiang, modern Shaanxi Province) to enter Sichuan and go as far as Chengdu; southward it passed through Hubei, Hunan, Guangxi, and ended at Guangzhou; northward it passed through Taiyuan to reach Fanyang (modern Beijing) and areas east of the Liaohe River in northeast China. As far as water transportation was concerned, the major artery between the north and the south was the Grand Canal. The Changjiang River was the most important water route in south China. Chinese ships could sail abroad from such places as Yangzhou and Guangzhou.

Strengthened Links Between Nationalities. Within the vast Tang empire, links between different nationalities were greatly strengthened.

The earliest home of the Turks was the Altay Mountains. By the middle decades of the sixth century when they became powerful, they controlled an area that extended eastward to Hinggan Mountains and westward to the Caspian Sea. They split into two groups, the east and the west, during the Sui Dynasty. Early during the Tang Dynasty, the aristocrats of the Eastern Turks often marched southward to creat difficulties in the border regions, and Emperor Taizong, time and again, sent troops to crush both groups. Later, the Tang government established in Qiuzi (Kuqa, modern Xinjiang) and Tingzhou (north of Jimsar, modern Xinjiang) the Anxi and Beiting Garrison Commands, respectively, that had jurisdiction over the vast areas north and south of the Tianshan Mountains. From then on, the economic and cultural exchange between the hinterland and these areas became more active.

The Mohe tribe was an offspring of the Sushen tribe and the ancestor of modern Manchus. Its members lived in the valleys of the Heilong, Songhua, and Wusuli rivers and also on the Sakhalin Island. It was divided into dozens of sections, of which Heishui and Sumo were the strongest. The Tang government named the chief of the

Heishui section, that had traditionally resided in the lower valley of the Heilong River, head of a new post known as the Heishui Garrison Command that had control of the middle and lower sections of the Heilong valley. It not only inaugurated a fairly comprehensive administration along the entire Heilong River valley but also brought the area closely together with the hinterland. Towards the end of the seventh century, Dazuorong, chief of the Sumo section inhabiting the Wusuli valley, unified all the neighbouring tribes and established a new regime. The Tang government, in response, appointed him head of the Garrison Command of Huhan Province centred around modern Tunhua, Jilin Province, and titled him Prince of Bohai Prefecture. The Sumo Mohe sent their talented men to Changan to study, and the returned students brought with them many books in the Han language. They exported to the hinterland such products as sable hides and ginseng roots.

There are many minority nationalities in Yunnan. Early during the Tang Dynasty, those residing around Erhai Lake were collectively known as the "Six Zhao", comprising six separate groups. They were, in fact, the ancestors of modern Yi and Bai nationalities. Of the six groups, Nanzhao, also known as Mengshezhao, was the strongest; later it decided to pledge fealty to the Tang government. After Piluoge, chief of Nanzhao, brought all the other five groups under his control, Emperor Xuanzong titled him King of Yunnan. The establishment of the Nanzhao regime helped the development of the Yunnan area and increased the contact between the various nationalities there.

The Tufans were the ancestors of modern Tibetans. Early in the seventh century, an outstanding Tufan leader named Songtsan Gambo unified all the tribes on the Qinghai-Tibet Plateau. He requested a Tang princess as his wife, and Emperor Taizong granted his request by marrying Princess Wencheng to him. Entering Tibet, the princess brought with her a variety of vegetable seeds, handicraft products, and books on medicine and technology. From then on, Han technicians specialized in wine brewery, paper making, metal smelting, and spinning and weaving continued to arrive in Tibet, and the Tang court imported from Tibet gold vessels, agate articles, musk, horses, and other items. Meanwhile, the children of Tufan aristocracy were sent to study in Changan. During the reign of Emperor Zhongzong, another Chinese princess named Jincheng was married to the Tufan leader Chide Zugdan. From the time when Princess Wencheng arrived in Tibet, the economic and cultural relations between the two nationalities became closer and closer.

An-Shi Revolt. To strengthen its control over the vast empire, the Tang regime, during its early period, established the post of military governor-general in the border regions and in the strategic areas within China proper. From then on, the power of a military governor-general continued to increase until he was in charge of not only the military but also the financial and administrative affairs in the area within his jurisdiction.

In 755, An Lushan, the military governor-general of Pinglu (southwestern section of modern Liaoning and northeastern section of modern Hebei), Fanyang (area around modern Beijing), and Hedong (area around Taiyuan, modern Shanxi), together with his top assistant Shi Siming, started a rebellion against the Tang regime. This is known in history as the An-Shi Revolt. At the head of 150,000 men, the two rebels, starting at Jicheng,

passed through Hebei and Shanxi to attack Henan. An
Lushan assumed the imperial title at Luoyang and subsequently attacked and captured Changan. Emperor
Xuanzong (r. 712-756) fled to Sichuan in a hurry. Later,
the Tang generals Guo Ziyi and Li Guangbi, assisted by
a contingent of army of the Uygur nationality, recovered
Changan and Luoyang. The rebels finally were defeated
after eight years of war.

The An-Shi Revolt brought with it miseries.
Agriculture was virtually destroyed, and people left
home and became refugees. The central government
was considerably weakened, and the military governors-
general took advantage of this situation to enlarge their
armed forces and territories. As the central government
lost control of its garrison commanders, China was divided up among the regional lords. The Tang Dynasty raced
from strength to weakness, from prosperity to decline.

Peasant Wars Towards the End of Tang. During the
later part of the Tang Dynasty, members of the royal
house, noblemen, high officials, and landlords competed
with one another in grabbing more and more land. The
peasants, having lost their land, became either tenants
or homeless refugees who drifted from one place to
another seeking a livelihood. Tax was extremely heavy
during the late Tang Dynasty. The government demanded the payment of "green sprouts" tax before the harvest was even ripe. Furthermore, drought occurred time
and again in Shandong and Henan, and countless peasants
could not find a livelihood. Peasant uprisings exploded
as a result.

In 874, Wang Xianzhi led a group of peasants to
stage an uprising in Changyuan (in modern Henan Province). The very next year, Huang Chao did likewise in

Caozhou (north of Caoxian, modern Shandong Province).
Shortly afterwards, the two groups merged. After Wang
Xianzhi was killed in action, his following was taken
over by Huang Chao. Calling himself "Heaven-Storm-
ing Generalissimo", Huang Chao adopted a strategy of
mobile warfare, attacking the weak and avoiding the
strong. He led 100,000 men in passing across the Changjiang River and fought in Anhui, Jiangxi, and Fujian.
He went as far as Guangzhou. In 880, he, at the head
of 600,000 men, re-crossed the Changjiang River and
marched northward. He took Luoyang and then Tongguan. Unceremonially, the Tang emperor escaped to
Sichuan. In 881, Huang Chao and his peasant army
marched, in a grand style, into Changan where he established a peasant regime. Unfortunately, he did not
choose to engage in hot pursuit of the demoralized Tang
army, thus giving the latter the opportunity for regroup-
ing itself. The Tang army, assisted by the landlords'
militias, counter-attacked. Since the insurgents had
always conducted a mobile warfare, they had no bases
of operation to speak of. As the Tang army surrounded
Changan on all sides, the insurgents were cut off from
food supplies, and they had no hope of receiving any re-
inforcements. At this crucial moment, Zhu Wen, a
lieutenant of Huang Chao's, mutinied and surrendered
to the Tang government. In 883, the insurgents were
forced to withdraw from Changan. The next year,
Huang Chao was killed in Hulanggu, near Mt. Taishan.
But the remainder of his army continued to fight for a
number of years.

Though the peasant army led by Huang Chao was
defeated in the end, it had dealt a severe blow to the
Tang government and sped up its demise.

Five Dynasties and Ten Kingdoms. While fighting against Huang Chao, the military governors-general enlarged their power and influence. In the Huanghe River valley, the most powerful were Li Keyong in modern Shanxi and Zhu Wen in modern Henan. In south China, there were also military governors-general who acted independently because of the military forces they commanded. In 907, Zhu Wen, in collaboration with a big bureaucrat named Ya Yin, entered Changan and forced Emperor Aidi to abdicate on his behalf. The dynasty Zhu Wen founded was known in history as Later Liang, which was followed successively by Later Tang, Later Jin, Later Han, and Later Zhou. Jointly they are referred to by historians as the Five Dynasties, that covered a period of 53 years (907-960). The area under their control was principally the Huanghe River valley. With the exception of the Later Tang whose capital was Luoyang, the capital of the other four regimes was Kaifeng.

Meanwhile in south China, there were, in succession, such regimes as the Wu, the Southern Tang, the Wuyue, the Min, the Chu, the Nanping, the Former Shu, the Later Shu, and the Southern Han. These nine regimes and the Northern Han, located in the central section of modern Shanxi Province, are referred to by historians as the Ten Kingdoms.

Recurrent wars during the period of the Five Dynasties and Ten Kingdoms brought to the people nothing but miseries. The establishment of the Northern Song Dynasty put an end to these separate regimes and completed the unification of the Central Plains with the south.

Cultural Activities During the Period of Sui, Tang, and Five Dynasties. Buddhism was very popular during the Sui-Tang period. Towards the end of the Tang Dynasty, however, an anti-Buddhist movement appeared. Among the anti-Buddhist leaders were Han Yu and Fu Yi. Thinkers with a materialist bent included Liu Zongyuan (773-819) and Liu Yuxi (772-842), both of whom viewed the relations between heaven and man from a materialist point of view.

The development of literature reached a high point during the Tang period. Tang poetry, that reflects the life of that period, is a literary treasure worldwide. Extant Tang poems number approximately 50,000, written by more than 2,200 persons, including the famous trio of Li Bai, Du Fu, and Bai Juyi.

As a poet, Li Bai (701-762) was imaginative and uninhibited. He enthusiastically eulogized the beauty of the motherland and, in the meantime, described the toil of peasants with empathy. He was a master of romanticism.

Du Fu (712-770) personally experienced the transition from prosperity to decline of the Tang Dynasty, as he lived through the later part of Emperor Xuanzong's reign. His poetry, therefore, reflects the social contradictions and people's miseries of this period. He, as a master of realism, left a deep impression on the development of realistic poetry. He was as famous as Li Bai.

Bai Juyi (772-846) lived at a time after the Tang Dynasty had already declined. Greatly influenced by Du Fu, he was in sympathy with the common people who had suffered only too much. Many of his poems describe the seamy side of Chinese society. All of his poems were written in an easily understood style, though profound in meaning. They have always been popular.

The Tang Dynasty was equally distinguished in

.prose. Prose of the parallel form was most popular from the Wei-Jin to the early Tang period. The composition of parallel form requires not only a parallel development of phrases and sentences but also the right kind of combination in tones and rhymes. A composition of this gender looks neat and often beautiful, but it was, usually, empty in content. Naturally, many men of letters were dissatisfied, and they advocated a return to the ancient period of Zhou, Qin, and Han as far as writing style was concerned. After the middle era of the Tang period, the so-called ancient-style movement quickly became a major event among the literati. In this movement Han Yu (768-824) and Liu Zongyuan made the greatest contribution. Because of their support, the ancient style gradually became the most popular way of writing prose.

The field of history made headway during the Tang period. Emperor Taizong ordered the establishment of a history institute whose function it was to write and edit the Tang history as well as the history of the previous dynasties. Among the latter were *History of the Jin Dynasty*, *History of the Liang Dynasty*, *History of the Chen Dynasty*, *History of the Northern Qi Dynasty*, *History of the Zhou Dynasty*, and *History of the Sui Dynasty*. In addition, there were histories written privately without government patronage or support, such as *History of the Southern Dynasties* and *History of the Northern Dynasties*. As for historical criticism, there was an excellent book entitled *On the Writing of History* by Liu Zhiji. *On Institutions* by Tu You dealt exclusively with political and economic institutions.

The fine arts was another field where great progress was made. There was a large number of distinguished painters, specialized in the painting of human figures, landscapes, flowers and birds, beasts and fowls, etc. Yan Liben and Wu Daozi were specialized in figure painting, and their depiction was live and realistic. Wang Wei was known for his landscapes, and his works were noted for their simplicity and elegance.

In sculpture, the Tang Dynasty left behind many works of excellence. Though the sculptured works inside the Longmen Grottoes of Luoyang dated back to the period of Emperor Xiaowen of the Northern Wei, the Tang Dynasty supplied the largest number of statues. The statue of Buddha in the Fengxian Temple looks serene and heroic, and it is as tall as 12.66 metres. The Mogao Grottoes in Dunhuang are also called Thousand Buddha Grottoes. The extant caves that have murals or statues in them number 492, of which 95 dated back to the Sui Dynasty and 213 originated in the Tang Dynasty. The latter figure proves beyond any doubt that the Tang Dynasty was one of the most glorious eras in cave sculpture.

The Tang Dynasty's achievement in calligraphy was equally impressive. Many famous calligraphers emerged, and jointly they made a great impact on the development of Chinese calligraphy. Among them were Yu Shinan, Ouyang Xun, Chu Suiliang, Yan Zhenqing, and Liu Gongquan.

Science and technology also made great progress during this period.

The art of printing was invented by the labouring masses of China. Block printing was invented during the Sui Dynasty, and by the Tang Dynasty the use of printing for the manufacturing of farmer's almanac, calendar, medical books, and model calligraphy had become commonplace.

In astronomy, a Buddhist monk named Yixing (Zhang Sui, 683-727, before his ordainment as a Buddhist monk), with the collaboration of Liang Lingzan, invented an instrument for the purpose of locating stars. He was the first man in history who discovered that "a fixed star moves by itself". He also initiated the measurement of the meridians from the earth.

As far as architecture was concerned, the Tang Dynasty followed the good tradition of the Western Han Dynasty and absorbed foreign technology. Cities, palaces, and temples were all constructed in a serene but elegant style. The capital of Changan had a circumference of more than 35 kilometres, and inside the city there were more than 20 avenues and streets, all of which, broad and straight, were planted with willows on both sides. The avenues and the streets crisscrossed, and the city map looked like a chessboard. The entire city was divided into more than 100 blocks. The magnificent palace was located in the northern section; for shopping, there were the Eastern and Western Markets. In the southern section of the city was the Dayan Pagoda inside the Daci'en Temple. It had seven stories and measured 64 metres in height. Standing majestically, it was a sight to see.

The Tang Dynasty was equally noted for its achievement in medicine. The Imperial Academy of Medicine was so specialized that it had departments of general medicine, acupuncture, massage, etc. Each department had its own professors and students. The department of general medicine was in turn divided into five sections, including internal medicine and surgery.

Principal Tang medical works included *One Thousand Golden Prescriptions, One Thousand Supplementary Golden Prescriptions, Medical Secrets on Contagious Diseases,* and *New Materia Medica of the Tang Dynasty.* Written by Sun Simiao, the first two were rich in content, having in them many ancient prescriptions. *Medical Secrets on Contagious Diseases* was written by Wang Tao; recording 21 categories of contagious diseases, it was the first book of this kind in Chinese history. *New Materia Medica,* compiled by Su Jing and others, recorded 844 herbs that could be used for medical purposes. It also corrected many mistakes found in some other pharmaceutical works.

Economic and Cultural Exchange with Other Asian Countries. Economic prosperity, cultural advance, and convenience in transportation all helped the economic and cultural exchange between China of the Tang Dynasty and many other Asian countries.

Changan, capital of the Tang, had as its residents not only ambassadors from different countries but also foreign merchants, students, monks, scholars, artists, and officials. They brought with them their native cultures which, infused with the Tang culture, made the latter even more brilliant. Meanwhile, they studied and absorbed what Tang China had to offer, which, eventually, helped the development of their own respective cultures.

Early during the Tang Dynasty, there were three states on the Korean Peninsula: Kokuli in the north, Paikche in the southwest, and Silla in the southeast. Silla unified the peninsula during Emperor Xuanzong's reign; it continued to maintain friendly relations with the Tang regime and sent its students to study in China. In the year 840 alone, there were 105 Silla students who, having finished their education in China, returned to Korea. They played an important role in spreading Chinese culture after returning home. Economic exchange between China and Korea was also frequent. The Koreans sent their horses, cattle, cloth, jute, drugs, and folding fans in exchange for Chinese silk, tea, porcelain, and embroideries. China also imported from Korea songs, dances, and musical instruments, all of which enriched the life of the Tang people.

Beginning with the Han Dynasty, the relationship between China and Japan continued without interruption. During the two centuries between 630 and 838, Japan sent 13 delegations to China. Members of each delegation could be as many as 500-600 persons, or at least 250 persons. Other than diplomatic envoys, retainers, and sailors, there were in each delegation students, learned monks, physicians, painters, musicians, and craftsmen. They studied Chinese politics, law, philosophy, Buddhism, literature and art, astronomy, calendar making, medicine, architecture, craftsmanship, etc. They exercised a fair influence on the development of Japanese politics, society, and culture.

In the cultural exchange between China and Japan, students and monks played a very important role. A Japanese student named Kibino Makibi studied in China for 17 years (717-734) and made considerable contribution in the fields of classics, history, law, and technology. He brought with him many Chinese books on his return to Japan. He contributed greatly to the development of Japanese institutions, calendar making, and music. There was another Japanese student named Abeno Nakamaro who arrived in China in 717 and adopted the Chinese name of Chao Heng. He served in the Tang court until 770 when he died in China. He was a close friend of such Tang poets as Wang Wei and Li Bai.

During the Tang Dynasty, many Chinese went to Japan, and the most famous among them was Jian Zhen, a noted Buddhist scholar. In 743, he was invited by Japanese monks to sail eastward. He tried six times in more than 10 years; finally, he arrived in Japan in 754 when he was 67 years old. He took with him many Buddhist scriptures. Once in Japan, he helped identify many herbs for medicine. He wrote a pamphlet on "secret prescriptions". Under his direction, a Buddhist temple named Toshodai was built in Nara with many Buddhist statues. From this temple, he helped promote the Tang architecture and sculpture. His own statue, made for him by his disciples, is still preserved in this temple. His statue and the temple symbolize the friendly relations between China and Japan.

India, Pakistan, and Bangladesh were jointly known as Tianzhu during the Tang Dynasty. Buddhism and the Tianzhu style of sculpture made their appearance in China at a very early time. In 641, Tianzhu sent a goodwill mission to China, and the Tang regime reciprocated by sending one itself. From then on, the exchange was frequent. Tianzhu medicine, astronomy, calendar making, linguistics, and music were absorbed by China, while Chinese paper and the technology of its manufacture spread to Tianzhu. The Chinese input helped the development of Tianzhu culture.

To study Buddhism more thoroughly, the famous Tang monk Xuanzang left China for Tianzhu in 627. He passed through today's Gansu, Xinjiang, and Central Asia and arrived at his destination after much ordeal.

He stayed in Tianzhu for 15 years, visiting famous temples and learning as much as he could from famous monks. He brought back more than 600 volumes of Buddhist scriptures and then proceeded to translate them. He and his disciples, according to what they had observed during their journey, wrote *Records of the Western Regions During the Tang Dynasty*, which recorded the geography, history, and customs of such places as Central Asia, Afghanistan, India, Pakistan, Nepal, and Sri Lanka. The book was and still is a valuable historical document.

In 671, another monk named Yijing left Guangzhou for India by the sea route and visited more than 30 countries in 25 years. He returned to Luoyang in 695, again by the sea route. He brought back to China 400 Buddhist scriptures. To introduce the religious and cultural life of India and other South Asian countries and also the accomplishments of many Chinese monks who had gone to Tianzhu for the same purpose as his, he wrote *Travel to Seek Buddhist Scriptures from the South Sea Region* and *Distinguished Tang Monks on Scripture-Seeking Travels to the Western Regions*. Both works are of enormous historical importance.

Other South and Southeast Asian countries also had close relationship with China during the Tang period.

Simultaneously, China's relationship with countries in West Asia, Europe, and Africa made good progress during this period. Persia, Tazi (Arabia), and the Eastern Roman Empire sent goodwill missions to China. During the period from 651 to 798, Tazi alone sent more than 30 goodwill missions.

Many famous Chinese cities of this period had Persian and Arab merchants, students, artists, and missionaries as residents. Many of these merchants, as well as students, chose to stay in China permanently, trading in silk and jewels. In the city of Yangzhou alone, there were several thousand Persian and Arab merchants. There were even more in Guangzhou, reportedly numbering tens of thousands. It was during the Tang Dynasty that Zoroastrianism, Manichaeism, Nestorianism, and Islam came to China. Foreign dances, music and acrobatics also came to China at this time. In recent years, silver coins from Persia, gold coins from the Eastern Roman Empire, and other relics of foreign origin were unearthed at Hejia Village, Xi'an, Shaanxi Province. The discovery indicates that the Chinese people had a friendly relationship with West Asian and European people during the Tang Dynasty.

Meanwhile, Chinese silk, art-craft products, and other culturally valuable items were exported to West Asia and Europe in large quantities via the Silk Road. The technology of making paper, weaving silk and manufacturing handicraft articles went to Africa and Europe by the route of Tazi. The input of Chinese culture contributed considerably to the cultural development of the countries concerned.

7. CONTINUAL DEVELOPMENT OF FEUDAL ECONOMY: LIAO, SONG, WESTERN XIA, KIN AND YUAN DYNASTIES (960-1368)

Establishment of Northern Song Dynasty. Social economy was severely damaged during the Five Dynasties when war went on almost uninterrupted. In 960, Zhao Kuangyin (927-976), commander of the imperial guards under the Later Zhou, mutinied and declared himself emperor. The new regime was Song, referred to by historians as Northern Song (960-1126), and its capital was Kaifeng, also known as Bianjing. Zhao Kuangyin was none other than Emperor Taizu who unified most of China after having successfully ended several local regimes.

During its early period, the Northern Song Dynasty took several measures to prevent the re-emergence of separatist local regimes so as to concentrate all power in the central government. The authority hitherto belonging to the military governors-general was taken over by the central government, and only civil officials could be appointed heads in charge of military and administrative affairs on the local level. In important provinces a new post, known as "supervisor", was created to control further the reduced power of governors. The power of local finance was in the hands of "transport envoys", and only the Privy Council in the central government had the authority of moving troops from one place to another.

Agriculture and handicraft industry made further progress during the Northern Song period. Peasants in the Central Plains and north China, engaging in intensive farming, used crooked hoe for weeding, iron harrow for loosening and breaking earth, and iron plough for turning it over. In south China, water wheels equipped with wooden chains, or wooden or bamboo tubes, were widely used for irrigating fields, and the cultivation of paddy rice became widespread. The planting of cotton went as far south as Fujian and Guangdong, and important progress was also made in the cultivation of sugar cane and tea. Tea plantations could be seen in

Guangdong and Guangxi as well as in the Changjiang and Huaihe river valleys.

The amount of gold, silver, copper, iron, lead, and tin mined during the Song period exceeded the amount produced during the Tang Dynasty. The production of coal was particularly large. The fuel used to smelt iron was mostly coal, and the quality of iron thus produced was much improved. The Song porcelain was a famous handicraft product, and new techniques such as furnace transmutation and crazing were employed during the firing process. Then there were six famous kilns, namely, the Guan (in Bianjing, modern Kaifeng), the Ding (in Dingxian, modern Hebei Province), the Ru (in Linru, modern Henan Province), the Jun (in Yuxian, modern Henan Province), the Ge (in Longquan, modern Zhejiang Province), and Jingdezhen (modern Jiangxi Province). The word "Jingde" in the name of the last kiln was Emperor Zhenzong's reign title, corresponding to a period from 1004 to 1007. The technology of manufacturing textiles and building ships was also much improved.

The Song commerce was more flourishing than its Tang counterpart. Among the best known commercial cities were Bianjing, Chengdu, Xijing, Jiangling, Yangzhou, Guangzhou, Quanzhou, Hangzhou, and Mizhou (Jiaoxian, modern Shandong Province). Bianjing was the largest city during the Northern Song period, having a circumference of more than 20 kilometres. Streets and avenues crisscrossed, and large numbers of shops prospered. The extant *Riverside Scene at "Qingming" Festival* painted by Zhang Zeduan of the Song Dynasty, depicts busy commercial activities on both sides of the Bianhe River in Bianjing during the *Qingming* (Clear and Bright) Festival. Village markets were equally busy. Currency in circulation at the time of Emperor Shenzong (r. 1067-85) was 17 times as much as it was during the reign of Emperor Xuanzong of the Tang Dynasty. Meanwhile, paper currency appeared for the first time in Sichuan. During the reign of Emperor Zhenzong (r. 998-1022), 16 rich merchants in Sichuan jointly issued a paper currency of their own, known as *jiaozi*. In 1023, Emperor Renzong established a paper currency bureau, and from then on, the printing of paper currency became a government monopoly. *Jiaozi* was the oldest paper currency in China, and its appearance reflected the economic prosperity of the Song Dynasty.

Liao and Western Xia and Their Relations with Northern Song. During the 300 years following the period of the Five Dynasties and Ten Kingdoms, the four regimes of the Liao, the Song, the Western Xia, and the Kin coexisted with one another.

In north China, the Liao regime (916-1125), founded by the Qidan (Khitan) aristocracy, lasted more than 200 years. Its territory extended northward to the Heilong River valley, eastward to the sea, and southward to the northern section of modern Hebei. The Qidan tribe had long been active in the Xar Moron River valley, located on the upper reaches of the Liaohe River in today's Liaoning Province. It became more and more powerful throughout the Tang Dynasty, by the end of which it had emerged as a major force in north China. In 907, its leader Apochi unified all the Qidan groups. In 916, he established a new regime named Qidan (later changed to Liao) and declared himself emperor. His capital was Linhuangfu (near Bairin Left Banner, modern Liaoning Province). Later, the Liao army marched southward and extended the Liao territory to the northern sections of modern Hebei and Shanxi provinces.

In 979 and again in 986, the Liao army decisively defeated its Song counterpart. Both sides dispatched envoys to Chanzhou (Puyang, modern Henan Province) to negotiate for peace. The resulting treaty stipulated that the Northern Song pay an annual tribute of 100,000 taels of silver and 250,000 bolts of silk to the Liao regime.

In 1125, the state of Liao was conquered by the state of Kin. On the eve of Liao's capitulation, Yelüdashi, a member of its royal house, led the Qidan remnants westward and established a new regime called Western Liao in the western section of modern Xinjiang and part of Central Asia. Its capital was Husiwoerduo, located to the west of the Ili River and south of the Chuhe River. The Western Liao regime was conquered by Genghis Khan at a later date.

While the Northern Song and the Liao were fighting against each other, the Dangxiang tribe (a branch of the Qiang nationality), located in today's Ningxia, Gansu, and northwest Shaanxi, established the Western Xia regime (1038-1227). The regime was recognized by the imperial court as legitimate from the late Tang to the early Song period. In 1038, Li Yuanhao declared himself emperor and called his regime Great Xia, referred to as Western Xia by historians. Its capital was Xingqingfu (Yinchuan, modern Ningxia), and it followed the Song model as far as governmental institutions were concerned. It invented its own written language, modeled after the Han script. Western Xia and Song were engaged in war against each other several times, resulting in damages and miseries for both sides. In 1044, peace was finally reached; Li Yuanhao relinquished his imperial title and was then titled by the Song regime as Sovereign of Xia. Each year the Northern Song "granted" Xia a gift, consisting of 153,000 bolts of silk, 72,000 taels of silver, and 30,000 catties of tea. After the death of Li Yuanhao, the Western Xia regime became weaker and weaker until it was exterminated by Genghis Khan in 1227.

Though war was frequent, the Han people, the Qidan, and the Dangxiang continued to maintain a close economic and cultural relationship. Uninterruptedly, the Han sent their silks, grains, tea, medicines, porcelain, and books to the Liao and Xia regimes, and received in turn horses, cattle, camels, carpets and rugs, etc.

Wang Anshi's Reforms. The expansion of the armed forces and the bureaucracy, plus the annual "gifts" to the Liao and Western Xia regimes, meant that the Song government could not make both ends meet, that taxes must be constantly increased, and that peasants would be more ruthlessly exploited. Further impoverished, the peasants revolted. In 993, Wang Xiaobo and Li Shun of Sichuan raised the slogan of "equalizing wealth" and staged a rebellion. Their followers numbered tens of thousands, shaking the Northern Song regime to its foundation. The slogan they raised indicated the dissatisfaction the peasant masses felt about the landlords' greed and ruthless exploitation and the wish of reaping the fruits of their own toil. It showed that the peasant struggle had reached a new stage. Though the uprising was suppressed in the end, the crisis the Northern Song rulers faced was by no means over.

In 1069, Emperor Shenzong called to duty a man named Wang Anshi (1021-86) for the specific purpose of conducting reforms. The purpose was twofold: the prosperity of the nation and the strengthening of its defence; and the easing of class contradictions. It was hoped that the trend of the nation becoming poorer and weaker would be arrested or even reversed.

There were two categories in Wang Anshi's reforms, financial management and reorganization of the armed forces. In the former category were programmes for land measurement and tax equalization, equitable distribution aimed at price control, labour service exemption, pre-harvest loans, and construction of irrigation works. In the latter category were the *bao-jia* (tithing) programme, the horse-breeding programme, and the military training programme.

Historically speaking, Wang Anshi's reforms were progressive. While they were carried out, they dealt a blow to the special privileges of the big bureaucrats, big landlords, and big merchants. The government's income, agricultural production, and the nation's military strength all improved. But the purpose of the reforms was the forestalling of peasant revolts so as to strengthen the Song Dynasty's feudal rule. As they affected adversely their interest, the big landlords and bureaucrats, led by Sima Guang, strongly opposed them. After the death of Emperor Shenzong, Sima Guang became prime minister, and the reforms were abolished in toto. From then on, class contradictions sharpened, and the uprisings led first by Song Jiang and then by Fang La exploded.

Establishment of Kin Regime and Fall of Northern Song. While the Northern Song was employing all its might in the suppression of peasant uprisings, the Nüzhen tribe in China's northeast became stronger and stronger. Members of this tribe had long lived in the Heilong River valley; later, they were unified by one of their clans named Wanyan. In 1114, Akutta, head of the Wanyan clan, led the Nüzhen forces and succeeded in defeating a Liao army of 100,000 men. In 1115, he assumed the imperial title and established the Kin Dynasty (1115-1234). His capital was located at Huiningfu (to the south of Acheng, modern Heilongjiang Province), renamed Shangjing or Upper Capital. By this time, the Nüzhen tribe had already had its own written language.

After its formal establishment, the Kin regime continued to attack Liao, which it conquered in 1125 when it captured the last Liao emperor named Tianzuo. Then it began to attack the Northern Song on a grand scale. In 1127, it took the Song capital Bianjing and captured as prisoners-of-war Emperor Huizong and Emperor Qinzong, plus many high officials. The Northern Song regime came to an end. In the same year, Zhao Gou, a younger brother of Emperor Qinzong's, assumed the imperial title at Yingtianfu (located to the south of Shangqiu, modern Henan Province). Zhao Gou, from then on, was known as Emperor Gaozong. The new regime he headed was referred to by historians as Southern Song (1127-1279), with its capital located at Linan (modern Hangzhou).

Southern Song-Kin Confrontation. Emperor Gaozong did not have the courage to confront the Kin forces; he, consequently, continued to flee southward, in the hope that eventually he would be left alone. Meanwhile, the Kin forces had gained control of most part of north China. South and north of the Huanghe River, many popular anti-Kin groups emerged, and they undermined Kin's control in areas which it had already conquered. Furthermore, they made their enemy think twice before he would march relentlessly southward.

In the Southern Song itself, there were also many generals who resisted Kin's aggrandizement, and the most famous among them was Yue Fei (1103-42). A native of Tangyin (in modern Henan Province), he was born to a poor peasant family. Beginning his career as a petty officer, he, because of his valour and wisdom, repeatedly distinguished himself on the battlefield until, eventually, he became a principal anti-Kin general. The army he commanded was known as the Yue Army which, in collaboration with the anti-Kin volunteers in north China, recovered much of the lost territory. In 1140, in the battle fought at Yancheng (in modern Henan Province), he decisively defeated the cream of the Kin forces. Taking advantage of the new victory, he and his men marched steadily forward until they reached Zhuxianzhen, near modern Kaifeng. At this point, a feud developed among the Kin ranks, and the anti-Kin volunteers, in the meantime, had cut off the line of the Kin army's logistical support. In fact, Wuzhu, the Kin commander, was prepared to relinquish Kaifeng and flee northward. At this moment when victory was close at hand, the capitulationists, led by Emperor Gaozong and his prime minister Qin Hui, decided to sue for peace, being fearful that a victory would be disadvantageous to them personally and that the anti-Kin volunteers, once becoming powerful, would threaten their position as rulers. They relieved Yue Fei of his commandership and later killed him. In 1141, Southern Song and Kin reached a peace agreement which stipulated that the boundary between the two regimes would be at Dasanguan (located to the southwest of Baoji, modern Shaanxi Province) in the west and Huaihe River in the east. Southern Song would

acknowledge Kin's suzerainty and pay an annual tribute
of 250,000 taels of silver and 250,000 bolts of silk. A
confrontation between the two regimes was thus created.

**Rise of Mongols and Unification of China by Yuan
Dynasty.** The Mongols were a minority nationality in
China dating back to ancient times. Originally, they lived in the areas to the east of the Ergun River; later, they
spread across the Mongolia Plateau between the Outer
Hinggan Mountains and the Altay Mountains. They
were nomads, proficient in hunting, riding and archery.
During the later part of the 12th century, a leader of
theirs named Temujin unified all the Mongol tribes. In
1206, he was elected the Great Khan, or Genghis Khan
(1162-1227), and established the Mongol regime. Later,
he led his army southward for the purpose of attack. In
1215, he captured Kin's Zhongdu (Middle Capital) and the
vast area north of the Huanghe River. In 1227, he conquered Western Xia. In the process, he died of illness in the
Liupan Mountains. His son Ogdai succeeded him and, in alliance with Southern Song, exterminated the Kin regime in
1234. After the conquest of Kin, the Mongol army concentrated its effort on attacking Song. In 1260, Kublai declared
himself the Great Khan and, following the Han fashion,
changed the title of his regime from "Mongol" to "Yuan"
(1271-1368).   Kublai was none other than Emperor
Shizu (r. 1260-94).   In 1276, the Yuan army entered
Linan and captured alive the Song emperor and the empress dowager. The Song premier Wen Tianxiang,
together with Zhang Shijie and Lu Xiufu, supported
first Zhao Xia and then Zhao Bing as emperor and continued the resistance. In the end, they were defeated,
due to the enormous power of the Mongols.

The unification of China by the Yuan ended the

political division that began during the last years of
the Tang Dynasty. It helped the development of China
as a unified country of many nationalities. In the central
government, the highest administrative organ was the
Central Secretariat, while the Privy Council and the
Censorate were in charge of military affairs and supervision of government officials, respectively. Locally,
the highest administrative unit was province. For the
first time in Chinese history, the Tibet region was organ
ized as an administrative unit, directly under the control
of the central government. An inspector's office was installed in Penghu and had jurisdiction over Taiwan as
well as Penghu. Today's Xinjiang and the areas north
and south of the Heilong River were part of the Yuan empire. The links between the various nationalities in
China were strengthened, and the strengthened links
helped economic and cultural development and the unification of the motherland.

Dadu (Beijing) during the Yuan Dynasty was the
economic and cultural centre of China. Marco Polo, the
Venetian who once served as an official in the Yuan
court, spoke of the people in that city as "well-to-do".
He wrote that there were all kinds of goods in its market
and more than 1,000 cartloads of silk were shipped into
the city each day. No city in the world could be compared to Dadu in terms of unusual goods from foreign
countries and goods in general that were available, he
added.

Transportation and communication were excellent
during the Yuan Dynasty. Along the key lines of
transportation, the government established more than
1,300 postal stations. The Grand Canal that linked the
north to the south was repaired and extended, so that

rich cities in south China had direct access to Beijing. As for sea transportation, ships sailing from Liujiangang (Liuhe near Taicang, modern Jiangsu Province), at the mouth of the Changjiang River, would head directly for Zhigu (Tianjin) via the Yellow Sea and the Gulf of Bohai.

The blue-and-white porcelain was a product that appeared for the first time during the Yuan Dynasty. Huang Daopo, a woman peasant, made great contribution to the textile industry.

Peasant Wars Towards the End of Yuan Dynasty. The Yuan rulers forcibly took over large amounts of land from the peasants and distributed them among garrison troops and temples. Besides, taxes in terms of produce, as well as labour service, were extremely heavy. The rulers also appropriated peasants' horses for military purposes. Altogether, the peasants lost more than 700,000 horses in this manner. Many peasants in north China, after losing their land, became serfs to Mongol aristocracy. To sow discord among the various nationalities, the Yuan rulers divided all the people in the country into four classes. The highest class belonged to the Mongols, followed in order by the *semu* people (including the Western Xia people and the Uygurs in the northwest and those who had migrated to China from Central Asia), the Han people (including the Nüzhen, the Qidan, and the Bohai people), and the southerners (the Han people and other nationalities in south China). The purpose of this division was to prevent people of the other nationalities from forming a united front against the Mongols.

Cruel oppression by the Mongols precipitated the resistance on the part of all nationalities. In 1351, the Red Turban Army, led by Liu Futong, raised the standard of revolt in Yingzhou, modern Anhui Province, and peasants in many other places favourably responded. As soon as the revolt began, Liu Futong and his men moved northward along three routes. However, due to lack of co-ordination and dissipation of forces, the northward march ended in failure, and Liu Futong died as a result. One contingent, led by Zhu Yuanzhang, attacked and captured Jiqing (Nanjing, modern Jiangsu Province) in 1356. After more than six years of fighting, the Zhu Yuanzhang group became big and strong and eventually controlled the middle and lower valleys of the Changjiang River. Having his base in south China stabilized, Zhu Yuanzhang, in 1367, sent Xu Da and Chang Yuchun in a northward march. The two generals succeeded in capturing Dadu and overthrowing the Yuan regime. The peasant uprisings, which carried with them great historical significance, ended when one group of feudal landlords replaced another as rulers of China.

Culture During the Song-Yuan Period. Both literature and science made important strides during the Song-Yuan period, and three of China's greatest inventions, printing, gunpowder and the compass, underwent further development. Block printing flourished in the Song Dynasty, and the invention of the movable type by Bi Sheng in the middle decades of the 11th century created a new era for the printing press. During the Yuan Dynasty, a movable type could be made either of tin or of wood. Later, the invention spread eastward to Korea and Japan and westward to Egypt and Europe, making great contribution to the development of world culture.

Gunpowder, discovered first by alchemists in ancient China, was used for military purposes towards the end of the Tang Dynasty. During the Song period, the technology of making gunpowder was further improved, and new weapons, such as the powdered arrow, the fire-gun and a primitive kind of cannon, were invented. During the Yuan Dynasty, the knowledge of making gunpowder spread from China to Europe via the Arab world.

The Chinese discovered the magnetic property of lodestone during the Warring States Period when the magnetic "south-pointing needle" was invented. During the Northern Song Dynasty, artificial magnet made its first appearance. Since a magnet needle always moved in a north-south direction, the compass soon came about. During the Southern Song period, merchant ships from China, using the compass, often sailed to and from Japan, the Malay Archipelago, and India. As Arab and Persian merchants travelled often in these ships, they too learned the use of the compass which they soon introduced into Europe. Needless to say, the use of the compass helped the development of navigation.

In his monumental work *Notes from the Dream Stream Garden*, the Northern Song scientist Shen Kuo (1031-95) recorded the scientific achievements of ancient China as well as the results of his own research. In 1088, the Northern Song astronomer Su Song designed an automatic armillary clock powered by water. It proved to be the oldest astronomic clock in the world. The Yuan scientist Guo Shoujing (1231-1316), having studied the ancient calendar of China, compiled the "almanac calendar" which gave a year's correct length as 365.2425 days, missing the true figure by only 26 seconds. The Yuan agriculturist Wang Zhen wrote *Book of Farming*, which had more than 300,000 words. At the time, it was the last word on agricultural technology, forestry, animal husbandry, sideline occupations, fishery, and other related subjects. It showed what an advanced level China had attained in agricultural production. In medicine, the Song Dynasty produced many books, but the most memorable among them were those on acupuncture. In 1026, the royal physician Wang Weiyi cast in bronze a human statue, on which all the acupuncture points were indicated. The bronze model, plus his written work on acupuncture that consisted of three volumes, helped later acupuncturists enormously.

In philosophy, the predominant ideas belonged to the Rational School, whose representatives were Cheng Hao and Cheng Yi of the Northern Song and Zhu Xi (1130-1200) of the Southern Song period. They regarded "reason" or "heavenly reason" as the origin of the universe and the feudal order as an embodiment of the "heavenly reason", eternal and immutable. They condemned the demand, on the part of the labouring masses, for a better life as wicked "human desire", contrary to "heavenly reason". They wanted everyone to eliminate "human desire" so as to preserve "heavenly reason". Chen Liang (1143-94), a progressive thinker of the Southern Song period, severely criticized philosophers like Zhu Xi, whom he referred to as "apathetic and indifferent men" indulged in idle and empty talk. He stressed the importance of concrete deeds that benefited one's fellow men. "The important thing is for a man to have the will to better the world and restore order," he said. "Then he will be a hero, even though his deeds may not conform completely to reason".

In the field of history, Sima Guang (1019-86) presided over the editorial work of *History As a Mirror* covering a period of 1,362 years, from the period of the Warring States to the period of the Five Dynasties. Consisting of 294 volumes, it was a masterpiece, as the materials had been carefully chosen and the narrative was lively and moving. Yuan Shu, a Southern Song historian, grouped the contents of *History As a Mirror* according to events and created a new book entitled *Events in "History As a Mirror"*, which proved to be the first book of its kind. In addition, there were *General History* by the Southern Song scholar Zheng Qiao and *A General Survey of Chinese Institutions* by Ma Duanlin who lived during the later Song and early Yuan period. Both works were on a par with their predecessor *On Institutions* by Du You of the Tang Dynasty.

In literature, the Song Dynasty was most noted for poetry in the *ci* style and the Yuan Dynasty for music drama. *Ci* — a new form of poems with lines of varied lengths — was very popular during the Song Dynasty, and many famous *ci* poets emerged. Su Shi (1037-1101) made great contribution by extending the *ci* content and by writing in such a free, unconstrained style that his works created the impression of being heroic as well as elegant. During the Southern Song Dynasty, Lu You (1125-1210) and Xin Qiji (1140-1207) were equally famous as *ci* poets. They had participated in the anti-Kin struggle early during their career; their *ci*, consequently, were impassioned and full of pathos. The Song Dynasty was also famous for prose, and it produced such outstanding prose writers as Wang Anshi, Ouyang Xiu, Su Shi, Su Xun, and Su Zhe.

The Yuan Dynasty was the golden era for music drama and produced such playwrights as Guan Hanqing,

Wang Shifu, and Ma Zhiyuan. The extant works of Yuan drama number more than 160, out of a total of 500 or thereabouts. In addition, there are isolated pieces unrelated to a long drama. Guan Hanqing (c. 1213-97), a native of Dadu, wrote more than 60 dramas, of which only a dozen, including *Snow in Midsummer*, have survived.

The Song-Yuan period also produced many famous painters. The most celebrated among them, as far as the Northern Song Dynasty was concerned, were Dong Yuan, Li Cheng, and Fan Kuan. Painter Zhang Zeduan recorded the busy life of Kaifeng in a painting named *Riverside Scene at "Qingming" Festival*. The main stream of painting during the Yuan Dynasty was landscape.

8. SLOW DECLINE OF THE FEUDAL SYSTEM: MING AND QING DYNASTIES (1368-1840)

Politics of Early Ming Period. In 1368, Zhu Yuanzhang assumed the imperial title and founded the Ming Dynasty (1368-1644). His reign title was Hongwu, and his capital was Nanjing. Zhu Yuanzhang was also known as Emperor Taizu (r. 1368-98). After his death, his eldest grandson Zhu Yunwen succeeded him as Emperor Jianwen, since his eldest son Zhu Biao had long died. The new emperor ordered the reduction of military strength of all the feudal princes, and Zhu Di (r. 1403-24) or Prince Yan, who was Zhu Yuanzhang's fourth son, revolted and succeeded in capturing Nanjing. He ascended the throne as Emperor Chengzu and made Beijing his capital. The new emperor's reign title was Yongle.

To strengthen the power of the central government, the early Ming rulers abolished the offices of the Central

Secretariat and of the prime minister, and their power
was distributed among the Six Ministries of Personnel,
Rites, Finance, Military Affairs, Justice, and Public
Works. Jurisdictionally, the president of each ministry
was directly responsible to the emperor. There was the
Censorate, headed by the Left and Right Censors; it was
responsible for the supervision of government officials.
There was also the Office of the Grand Councillors.
Earlier, the councillors served as advisers to the emperor;
later, they assumed more and more power and respon-
sibility until eventually the head of the councillors became the de facto prime minister. On the local level, the
nation was divided into 13 provinces, each of which was
headed by a governor, responsible for civil affairs and
finance. In addition, each province had a judge responsible for the administration of justice and a commander
responsible for military affairs. Below the level of provinces there were prefectures and counties. In remote
regions and areas where minority nationalities were concentrated, a different type of administration, known as
garrison command, prevailed. The head of a garrison
command was in charge of military as well as civil affairs.

The Ming Dynasty continued the practice of select-
ing officials by examinations, a practice that began during the Sui-Tang period. Each prefecture, subprefecture
or county had its own school, a graduate of which, having
passed the required examinations, would receive a degree
known as *Xiu Cai* ("Flowering Talent"). A *Xiu Cai* could
participate in the provincial examination held at the provincial capital, and the winner would be referred to as
a *Ju Ren* ("Recommended Man"). A *Ju Ren* was entitled
to take the metropolitan examination held at the nation's
capital and, if he succeeded, would participate in the

palace examination personally supervised by the emperor. If he emerged successfully in the palace examination, he would receive the *Jin Shi* ("Advanced Scholarship") degree. Then he would be granted an official post to hold, either in the central government or on the local level. During the Ming Dynasty, the examination system was the main road to officialdom.

The Ming Dynasty built a huge army whose men were stationed in the various military areas controlled by the respective provincial commanders. At the central level, there were the Five Military Commands — the Front, the Rear, the Left, the Right and the Central — in charge of all the military areas. Nominally, the Ministry of Military Affairs alone had the power to move troops, though it had no troops under it. Supreme military power was in the hands of the emperor himself.

Outside the regular judiciary organs, the Ming government had also such extralegal organizations as Multicolour Guards, East Chamber, West Chamber, and Internal Chamber, that were specialized in information gathering, secret arrest, and clandestine trial. They were in fact secret police that kept a close watch on both officials and civilians whom they brutalized at will.

From time to time the government dispatched officials to the various parts of China to take census of land and population. The purpose was to exact more in terms of taxes and labour services and to exploit the people more effectively.

To promote agricultural production, especially the cultivation of cash crops, the government encouraged the opening up of wilderness and the construction of irrigation works.

The economic and political policies listed above

strengthened the early Ming regime.

Development of Social Economy and Nascent Capitalism. During the Ming Dynasty, both cultivated acreage and grain production increased by a sizable amount; this was especially true with regard to paddy rice. A number of devices — powered by oxen, men, or wind — were invented for farm irrigation. Then the cultivation of cotton had spread to the Huanghe River valley, and cotton, finally, replaced hemp as the basic material for making cloth. Huzhou, Zhejiang Province, was a famous city in the production of silk, and the name of "Huzhou Silk" was known throughout China. Silkworm-raising was also popular in other regions like Hubei, Hunan, Guangxi and Sichuan, and the areas north and south of the Huaihe River.

Mining and handicraft industry made headway too. Then iron-smelting as a private enterprise was quite common, and the technology involved was also very advanced. For instance, the iron-smelting furnace in Zunhua, Hebei Province, was as high as 12 feet and could handle more than one ton of ore each time. Its bellow was manned by 4-6 workers simultaneously; it could also make alloys. The bronze bell, housed in the Juesheng Temple (also known as the Big Bell Temple) in Zengjiazhuang on the western suburb of modern Beijing, was cast during the reign of Yongle. It is seven metres in height and 3.3 metres in circumference at its opening; it weighs as much as 43,500 kilogrammes. Buddhist scriptures running into more than 200,000 Chinese characters were inscribed inside and outside the bell. It is grand on scale and yet extremely refined.

Then the centres of the textile industry were Suzhou, Hangzhou, Jiaxing, and Huzhou. Porcelain kilns were usually large, and the technology of firing had been greatly improved. Jingdezhen was then the capital of the porcelain industry, and its products were known throughout the world. Paper making and printing were further developed, and shipbuilding was even more noticeable for its scale. The advanced technology in shipbuilding was clearly demonstrated in the ships that sailed for the "Western Ocean" under Zheng He's command early during the Ming Dynasty.

Side by side with agriculture and handicraft industry, commerce progressed by leaps and bounds. There were more than 30 famous cities across the country; they were centres of such industries as textile, food, tea, and printing. Along the coast were cities specialized in maritime trade, such as Fuzhou, Quanzhou, Guangzhou, and Ningbo. Cities specialized in the handicraft industry became prosperous too.

Silver was used as a medium of exchange before the Ming Dynasty, but its role was comparatively minor as the main medium of exchange was still copper coins. Early during the Ming Dynasty, certain parts of China began to accept silver for tax payments; from then on, it became more and more popular until eventually it became the principal medium of exchange. The use of silver as money indicated the increase of goods bought and sold as well as the enlargement of the market itself.

Beginning with the middle period of the Ming Dynasty, capitalist relations of production began to develop in the silk and cotton industries in China's southeast, as agriculture and handicraft industry continued to make progress and as commodity economy developed. There were several thousand textile workshops in the city of Suzhou alone, employing large numbers of workers. The division of labour in them was detailed, and production large. Among their workers were those who had nothing to sell except their labour power and technical skill since they did not own any looms. They "were able to earn a living when they were employed", but they "had no means of livelihood when they were out of job". Their relationship with their employers was one between labour and capital, very much a capitalist relationship. Then the natural economy, characterized by a combination of agriculture and handicraft industry, was still predominant. The capitalist relations of production, still in their early and infant stage, could not but grow slowly, being fettered by a feudal system.

Administration of Border Regions. During the Ming Dynasty, most inhabitants in the Heilong and Songhua valleys in China's northeast were the Nüzhens, but there were also some Han, Mongolians, Koreans, and other nationalities. In 1409, the Ming government established the Nurkan Garrison Command at Telin, where the Heilong River poured into the sea. It governed all the people in the region extending eastward to the Sakhalin Island, westward to the Onon River, southward to the Sea of Japan, and northward to the Oudi River and the Outer Hinggan Mountains. Within this vast region, the government established a number of military areas, all under the jurisdiction of the Nurkan Garrison Command.

In the Xinjiang region of China's northwest lived the Uygurs and some other minority nationalities, including the Han people. In this region the Ming government installed eight military areas, with a territorial jurisdiction that extended eastward to Jiayuguan, Gansu Province, westward to Lop Nur, northwestward to the

Barkol Mountains, and southwestward to the Qaidam Basin.

The Ming government established in Tibet, then known as Dbus-Gtsang, the Dbus-Gtsang Garrison Command, which had jurisdiction over all the military offices in the region.

As for certain areas of Yunnan and Guizhou where minority nationalities lived, the Ming government followed the Yuan practice by continuing the system of native offices, in which chiefs of these nationalities were appointed officials in charge of prefectures, subprefectures, and counties. Later, such officials were appointed directly by the central government — officials whom the government could dismiss or remove as it wished. The change helped the stability and development of the minority areas.

The Ming government, like its predecessor, established an inspector's office at Penghu which had jurisdiction over Taiwan as well as Penghu.

Peasant Uprisings Towards the End of Ming Dynasty. Governmental corruption went from bad to worse towards the end of the Ming Dynasty, as eunuchs and court officials competed with one another for more power and privileges. As the government became more chaotic, land grabbing became more intensive. Using the pretence that a war was going on in China's northeast and that soldiers must be recruited and trained to suppress peasant rebellion, the government resorted to all kinds of measures to exact money from the people. Facing this kind of exploitation and oppression, poor peasants were totally helpless when natural disaster struck. During the last 70 years of the Ming Dynasty, flood, drought, pestilence, and famine occurred repeatedly; fertile fields deteriorated into wilderness, and starvation was reported everywhere. Having been forced to choose between death and rebellion, the peasant masses did not hesitate to make up their mind.

In 1627, northern Shaanxi experienced a severe drought, and not one kernel of grain was harvested. Yet the government continued to pressure people for tax payment. As thousands of peasants died of hunger, those who had survived raised the standard of revolt. Peasants in other areas responded in sympathy. From Shaanxi and eastern Gansu emerged such peasant leaders as Gao Yingxiang, Li Zicheng, Zhang Xianzhong, and others who, jointly, commanded dozens of insurgent groups. Not only the Han but also the Mongolians and the Hui people participated in this revolutionary struggle.

In 1635, 13 leaders of the insurgents, commanding 72 battalions of troops, held a conference in Xingyang, Henan Province. The most outstanding among them were Li Zicheng (1606-45) and Zhang Xianzhong (1606-46). The group led by Li Zicheng fought in Shaanxi, Gansu, Sichuan, Hubei, and Henan, while Zhang Xianzhong and his men were active in Hubei and Sichuan.

Li Zicheng raised the slogan of "equal landownership and zero taxation", a slogan that reflected the poor peasants' pressing need. It also indicated that the peasant war had advanced to such a new stage that they, the peasants, actually demanded the change of China's feudal landownership to a better system. Wherever they went, Li Zicheng and his men were welcomed by the broad masses, and the insurgents quickly snowballed to hundreds of thousands. In 1644, they moved towards Beijing and met little resistance. In a little more than one month, they reached the capital, and the Ming troops, who were supposed to defend the city, surrendered one after another. Having no place to go, Chongzhen, the last Ming emperor, committed suicide by hanging himself at the Coal Hill (or Jingshan Hill). The grand army led by Li Zicheng entered Beijing, and the Ming Dynasty came to an end.

Not resigned to defeat, the remnants of the Ming forces, in collaboration with the Manchu aristocracy, continued to struggle against the peasant army.

Defeat of Peasant Army by Manchus. The Manchus constituted one branch of the Nüzhens. Early during the Ming Dynasty, the Nüzhens lived in the Songhua and Heilong river valleys, all under the jurisdiction of the Nurkan Garrison Command. During the later Ming Dynasty, they were placed under the unified leadership of a Nüzhen chief named Nurhachi. In 1616, Nurhachi assumed the title of Khan and established a new regime called Great Kin, referred to as Later Kin by historians. After his death, he was succeeded by his son Huangtaiji who, in 1636, called himself emperor and changed the dynastic title from "Great Kin" to "Great Qing". Huangtaiji was also known as Emperor Taizong of Qing who gradually unified all of China's northeast.

The Qing army was posed to invade China proper at the time when the peasant army led by Li Zicheng entered Beijing and ended the Ming regime. It was provided with a great opportunity for offensive action when the peasant army did not choose to eliminate all the Ming remnants or take effective measures for defence against a possible attack by the Qing forces. The Ming general Wu Sangui, then stationed at Shanhaiguan Pass, surrendered to the Qing army and led the latter to enter China proper. Jointly, he and his new master proceeded with the task of suppressing the peasant uprising. Without careful preparation for defence, Li Zicheng was forced to withdraw from Beijing. Later, he fought in Shanxi and Shaanxi. In May 1644, the Qing army entered Beijing. In September, Emperor Shunzhi (r. 1644-61), or Shizu, moved the Qing capital from Shenyang to Beijing. Efforts were then begun to unify all of China.

Subsequently, the Qing army attacked the peasant insurgents along two routes. Li Zicheng went from Shaanxi to Hubei where, at Mt. Jiugong in Tongshan, he was ambushed and killed by landlord militias. Zhang Xianzhong and his men fought in the middle valley of the Changjiang until the Qing army entered Sichuan and killed him.

Though the peasant army led by Li Zicheng and Zhang Xianzhong was in the end crushed by a coalition of Han and Manchu landlords, the surviving forces, led by Li Dingguo and Li Laiheng, continued the anti-Qing struggle for some time.

Meanwhile, many Ming bureaucrats, landlords, and members of the gentry also waged a war of resistance against the Qing for the protection of their own interests. They supported, successively, Prince Fu's regime (from May 1644 to May 1645) in Nanjing, Prince Lu's regime (from July 1645 to March 1653) in Zhejiang, Prince Tang's regime (from August 1645 to September 1646) in Fujian, and Prince Gui's regime (from November 1646 to May 1662) in Huguang and the southwest. Since all these regimes were located in south China, historians refer to them as the Southern Ming regimes. Most officials in these regimes, being corrupt, fought among themselves for selfish ends. The first three of these regimes were quickly exterminated by the Qing army.

Only Prince Gui's regime, thanks to the co-operation between some of its generals and the peasant insurgents, lasted a little longer.

Social Economy of Early Qing. Having succeeded in suppressing all the anti-Qing forces, the Qing leaders, step by step, unified all of China. The new regime inherited and developed further the feudal autocracy of its predecessor. Emperor Yongzheng set up a Privy Council, and he personally selected some Manchu princes, grand councillors, and ministers and deputy ministers of the Six Ministries as members. In local administration, the largest unit was province, headed by a governor. More powerful than a governor was a governor-general, who had under his jurisdiction one, two, or sometimes three provinces. Both the governor and the governor-general were in charge of military as well as civil affairs. Below the provincial level were circuit, prefecture, subprefecture, county, and district. At the bottom of the administrative structure were the *bao* and the *jia*, the two making up a tithing system. The highest officials were mostly members of the Manchu aristocracy, but there were also some Han people and leaders of the minority nationalities who reached the top.

The Qing army comprised the garrisons of the Eight Banners (Manchu troops) and the Green Battalions (of Han origin). Numbering 220,000 men, the former were stationed in Beijing and its vicinity as well as the strategic points across the country. The Green Battalions, so named because they used green insignias, totalled nearly one million and were placed under the various regional commanders.

Following the Ming example, the Qing government, in 1646, made public *The Qing Code*. Later, elaboration by examples was added, and the new volume was called *Elaboration of the Qing Code.*

To strengthen its rule, the Qing government adopted policies aimed at the ease of social contradictions and the recovery of economic production. Emperor Kangxi (r. 1662-1722) ordered the cessation of land aggrandizement, while proclaiming, "There would be no additional poll tax regardless of the increase in population". Besides, the poll tax was merged with the land tax which only landowners had to pay. The conversion of the poll into a levy on land was in fact the continuation of the single tax system practised during the Ming Dynasty. In the single tax system, different tax exactions, including part of the poll, and all the labour services were combined to form one levy, to be paid in silver. Towards the end of the Ming Dynasty, however, extralegal levies were added, and they became heavier and heavier with the passage of time. As a result, the so-called single tax existed in name only. What the Qing government did was to implement the essentials of the single tax system, plus some improvement.

During Emperor Yongzheng's reign (1722-35), the policy of converting the poll to a levy on land was carried out throughout the country, benefiting the development of social economy enormously. Wasteland was cultivated, and agricultural production gradually increased. There was also an increase in population. According to the Qing government's own statistics, the amount of land under cultivation was only 2.9 million *qing* (one *qing* = 100 mu) in 1651, and the population, in the same year, was only 10.6 million. In 1761, the land figure increased to 7.4 million *qing*, and the population, in 1764, was more than 200 million.

Commerce prospered along with the increase of population and agricultural production. Large textile factories could be found in Jiangning (Nanjing), Suzhou, Hangzhou, and other cities. During Emperor Qianlong's reign (1736-95), the city of Jiangning alone had more than 30,000 silk looms. The looms themselves had also undergone changes for the better. In 1730, there were more than 19,000 cloth stampers in the city of Suzhou. The technology of smelting iron made further progress, and a furnace in some places could produce anywhere from 1,500 to 2,000 kilogrammes of pig iron per day. The highest on record was 3,000 kilogrammes per day. Copper mining in Yunnan was developed rapidly; during Emperor Qianlong's reign there were more than 300 copper mines in that province. As for the making of porcelains, the city of Jingdezhen employed several hundred thousand porcelain workers. Progress was also made in the shipbuilding, sugar refining, paper making, tobacco, and dyestuff making industries.

During the reigns of Kangxi, Yongzheng, and Qianlong, cities became more and more prosperous. By then Beijing had become the trade centre of China. Merchants from different provinces organized their own guilds with offices in large cities. As commerce developed, nascent capitalism grew slowly but steadily. In the handicraft industry, buying for the purpose of reselling was very active, and the number of handicraft factories organized in the capitalist fashion increased as a result. Money houses specialized in deposit acceptance, lending, and remittance made their first appearance early during the Qing Dynasty. Still, the development of capitalism was severely fettered by the feudal system. The Qing government persisted in pursuing an anti-commercial policy and, by repeated orders, forbade citizens to open mines on their own. It even put a limit on the number of looms a factory could own. Besides, it imposed burdensome taxes, so burdensome in fact that many merchants were forced to close shops as they became bankrupt. It was no surprise that capitalism could not develop under these circumstances. Across the country, the self-sufficient, natural economy still dominated.

Unification of Multi-national China Consolidated. All nationalities within China jointly created and developed a great civilization. During the Qing Dynasty, more than 50 nationalities — the Han being the most numerous — lived within the boundary of China, and the relations between them were closer than ever. The Qing government established in the capital the Board of Minority Nationalities Affairs specially responsible for the administration of the border regions where such nationalities were concentrated. Generals and ministers were dispatched there to handle military and administrative affairs on behalf of the central government.

Towards the end of the 17th century, three times the Qing government sent troops to attack the Jungar Mongolian tribe west of the desertland on the Mongolia Plateau and succeeded in pacifying the region. During the reign of Qianlong, it also succeeded in pacifying and then unifying the Xinjiang region where the reactionary aristocracy had revolted. An office of the Ili General was installed, and the office had jurisdiction over all areas north and south of the Tianshan Mountains. The Qing government also stationed troops in various places in Xinjiang, thus strengthening the defence of the northwestern frontier.

The Qing Dynasty inherited jurisdiction over Tibet

from the Ming Dynasty. Shortly after its establishment, the Qing government received from Dalai Lama and Bainqen Lama, rulers of Tibet, the pledge of fealty. Later, it sent to Tibet a resident minister who, representing the central government, managed Tibetan affairs and appointed local officials jointly with the two lamas. It also increased garrison troops in Tibet.

As for its policy towards the minority nationalities in China's southwest such as the Miao, the Yao, and the Yi, the Qing government followed the practice of its predecessor by appointing, as many as possible, government officials to replace native chiefs as local administrators. As the independence or semi-independence on the part of native chiefs was, basically speaking, terminated, the defence of the southwestern region was strengthened.

There are in the South China Sea more than 200 islands that fall into four groups: Dongsha Islands, Xisha Islands, Zhongsha Islands, and Nansha Islands. During the Qing Dynasty, these islands maintained closer relations with the Chinese mainland, and those who came from the mainland for a visit were numerous. Written records about these islands continued to appear. Both *The Atlas of the Royal Provinces of the Qing Dynasty* (1755) and *The Atlas of the Great Unified Qing Empire* (1817) had these islands on their maps.

The Chinese territory, as defined by maps of the early Qing period, included the Nansha Islands in the south, and Taiwan and its adjacent islands in the southeast. In the northeast, it extended to the Outer Hinggan Mountains and the Sakhalin Island. Northward it bordered on Siberia, and northwestward it reached the northern shore of Lake Balkhash. In the west, it reached the Pamirs. Other than the prefecture of Shuntian and the former capital of Shengjing, there were the following 18 provinces: Zhili (Hebei), Shandong, Shanxi, Henan, Shaanxi, Jiangxi, Anhui, Zhejiang, Jiangsu, Yunnan, Guizhou, Gansu, Sichuan,· Hubei, Hunan, Guangdong, Guangxi, and Fujian. In addition, there were the following border territories: Inner Mongolia, Qinghai Mongolia, Khalkha Mongolia, Tannu-Ulanhai, Xinjiang, and Tibet.

Culture During the Ming-Qing Period. The Ming-Qing period witnessed great achievement in science and culture. The great pharmaceutist Li Shizhen (1518-93) wrote *Materia Medica,* which records more than 1,800 different herbs and more than 11,000 prescriptions. The book has been translated into English, French, German, Japanese, Latin, Korean, and other foreign languages. Scientist Song Yingxing (1587-c. 1660), who flourished towards the end of the Ming Dynasty, summarized all of China's experience in agriculture and the handicraft industry by writing *Exploitation of the Works of Nature,* which reflects the level of science and technology of his time. About the same time there was a geographer named Xu Hongzu (1586-1641) who travelled across the country to study mountains and rivers. He wrote *Travels of Xu Xiake* that, among other things, describes in detail the erosion of limestone by water and the resulting landform in China's southwest.

Among the more progressive thinkers of the Ming period was Li Zhi (1527-1602) who subjected feudal ethics to severe criticism and opposed strongly discrimination against· the female sex. Wang Fuzhi (1619-92), who lived during the late Ming and early Qing period, insisted that the universe, composed of matter, was not created by god or gods. He believed that spirit, originated in matter, could not exist without matter. He believed in historical progress and opposed the return to ancient times. Another progressive thinker of the same period was Huang Zongxi (1610-95) who opposed and criticized the corrupt system of feudal autocracy which, he believed, was the root cause of chaos in the world. All these thinkers exercised some influence on the bourgeois democratic revolution.

In literature, the Ming-Qing period produced several outstanding novels. Among them were *Romance of the Three Kingdoms* by Luo Guanzhong (c. 1330-1400), *Outlaws of the Marsh* by Shi Nai'an, *Journey to the West* by Wu Chengen (c. 1500-82), and *A Dream of Red Mansions* by Cao Xueqin (c. 1715-64). The last-mentioned is also the best. It describes the love, marriage, and tragedy involving three persons: Jia Baoyu, Lin Daiyu, and Xue Baochai. As it portrays the rise and fall of a feudal aristocratic family, it also reveals the corruption and decadence of feudal society. Pu Songling (1640-1715) wrote a collection of short stories entitled *Strange Tales from a Carefree Studio*, and Wu Jingzi (1701-54) was the author of a long satire known as *The Scholars*. Both have been highly praised for their literary merit. In drama, the outstanding works were *The Peony Pavilion* by Tang Xianzu (1550-1617), *The Palace of Eternal Youth* by Hong Sheng (1645-1704) and *The Peach Blossom Fan* by Kong Shangren (1648-1718).

Foreign Relations During the Ming-Qing Period. China played an active role in its relations with foreign countries during the Sui, Tang, Song, and Yuan dynasties, but it became passive during the Ming-Qing period. At a time when the Ming Dynasty was replaced by the Qing Dynasty and when China remained feudal and in-

ert, capitalism rose dynamically in the West. Worse
still, Chinese rulers were totally ignorant of the world
situation as it then developed. Beginning in the first
decades of the 16th century, some of the Western countries moved eastward to proceed with their colonial activities and encroached upon Chinese territories in the
process. Later, their ambition regarding China became
bigger and bigger. It is true that China showed its own
exuberance early during the Ming Dynasty when it sent
Zheng He (1375-1435) and his flotilla to visit many Asian
and African countries and that early during the Qing
Dynasty it launched counter-attacks against the aggressors from tsarist Russia. Yet, the position of China had
become more and more passive on the whole.

To develop China's relations with foreign countries,
Emperor Chengzu (Zhu Di) of Ming and his successors
dispatched Zheng He to visit and trade with many of
the Asian and African countries. Altogether Zheng He
made seven voyages. He visited Indochina, the Malay
Archipelago, India, Iran, and Arabia. He went as far as
the eastern coast of Africa. Altogether he visited more
than 30 countries over a period of more than 20 years.

Zheng He's voyages helped the economic and cultural exchanges between China and many Asian and
African countries; they also enhanced the friendship
between the Chinese people and the people of these
countries. From then on, more and more Chinese migrated to Southeast Asia for permanent settlement. These
Chinese brought with them farming skills, iron tools,
bronze articles, and the technology of making porcelain,
refining sugar, and planting tea. Together with the na-

tives, they made great contribution to the economy and culture of the countries where they lived.

For two centuries beginning in the early Ming Dynasty, Japanese pirates frequently raided China's southeastern coast, killing and plundering. They sometimes attacked and captured cities and brought about enormous damages. The situation for coastal defence changed for the better, however, when a general named Qi Jiguang (1528-87) emerged. With the support of the broad masses and of local authorities, the general, from 1561 to 1565, repeatedly defeated these pirates in Zhejiang, Fujian, and Guangdong.

During the late Ming and early Qing period, the colonialists from Holand and Spain invaded and occupied the southern and northern sections of Taiwan at one time or another. Later, the Dutch succeeded in chasing the Spaniards out from the island. The cruel oppression and ruthless exploitation of the Taiwanese by the Dutch colonialists precipitated strong resistance on the part of the Chinese people. In 1661, the anti-Qing general Zheng Chenggong (1624-62) and his men sailed from Xiamen and Jinmen towards Taiwan. With the support of the Taiwan people, he succeeded in chasing out the Dutch colonialists. He set up a regime in Taiwan, which persisted until 1683 when the Qing army attacked and made Taiwan part of the Qing empire. The Qing government installed a prefectural office in charge of the island's administration and stationed troops there for the purpose of defence. From then on, the economic and cultural relations between the mainland and Taiwan became closer and closer.

Tsarist Russia was a European country, far away from China. In the 16th and 17th centuries, it expanded eastward and occupied the vast territory in Siberia. It soon directed its aggression towards China. Beginning in 1643, it invaded China's Heilong River valley, burning and killing. It occupied such cities as Yacsa and Nipchu. In response, Emperor Kangxi resolutely counter-attacked so as to check tsarist Russia's ambition of expansion. In 1689, the Treaty of Nipchu was concluded on the principle of equality. The eastern boundary between the two countries was delineated at Gorbitza River, the Erhkuna (Ergun) River, and the Outer Hinggan Mountains eastward right to the sea. The areas south of the Outer Hinggan Mountains and east of the two rivers were Chinese territories. Legally and officially, the treaty affirmed that the vast area of the Heilong River valley and the Wusuli River valley, including the Sakhalin Island, belonged to China.

In the 16th century, some of the European countries had reached the stage of primitive capitalist accumulation, and the colonialists began to plunder overseas. The first European arrivals in the Orient were the Portuguese. In 1511, they conquered Malacca and began to raid the coastal areas of China's Guangdong Province. They were repulsed, however, by the Ming troops and people. In 1553, the Portuguese, by bribing local Chinese officials, occupied part of Macao in the name of having obtained a lease. In 1557, they illegally enlarged their occupied territory in Macao and began to establish administrative offices and build fortifications. They, in fact, regarded Macao as their colony. Macao turned out to be the first piece of Chinese territory illegally occupied by a Western power. However, China continued to maintain its own administration in Macao and thus maintained its sovereignty over the place.

In the wake of the Portuguese came the Spanish and Dutch colonialists. Their invasion of the Chinese territory Taiwan has been mentioned earlier.

During the 17th and 18th centuries, the capitalists of Britain, France, and the United States energetically expanded their overseas markets. In terms of commercial plundering and colonial expansion, none was more ambitious than Britain. In 1600, the British colonialists founded the East India Company. In 1699, they established in Guangzhou a trading establishment (then called "factory") which brought the influence of the East India Company to China. In 1793, a special envoy from Britain named Macartney (Lord George) arrived in China, requesting the privilege of trading in Zhoushan Island, Ningbo, Tianjin, and some other places. The request was denied. Then the Qing government, having in mind the strengthening of feudal control, adopted a closed-door policy in so far as foreign trade was concerned, and it designated only one city, namely, Guangzhou, as a trading port. The British sold to the Chinese woollens and spices, while buying from China such items as tea, silk, medicine, and porcelain. Beginning in the second decade of the 19th century, cotton textiles became the major item of British export to China. However, owing to China's closed-door policy and its self-sufficient, natural economy, British sales in the Chinese market were never large. In fact, British trade with China was negative or unfavourable. To reverse the negative balance of trade, the British colonialists began to ship large quantities of opium to China. The peddling of poison by the British colonialists not only destroyed the health and the will of millions of Chinese but also caused the outflow of large quantities of silver which, in turn, created a financial crisis for China. From the Chinese point of view, the trade in opium must be stopped; from the British point of view, it must be maintained in order to continue to realize huge profit. The contradiction eventually led to war that exploded in 1840.

Side by side with the Western plunder, Western missionaries came to China to teach Christianity. In fact, missionary activities were merely another espect of imperialist aggression. Beginning in 1579, Jesuits arrived in China in Western ships. During the late Ming and early Qing period, they established Catholic churches in 13 of China's provinces. In 1610, there were 2,500 Catholic converts in China; the number was 150,000 in 1650. Taking advantage of their daily contact with the Chinese people and of the opportunity of serving the Chinese government, the missionaries collected intelligence which they forwarded to the colonialists for the benefit of the latter's aggressive activities. Around the time of the Opium War of 1840, there were Protestant as well as Catholic missionaries in China, all of whom participated directly in aggression against the country.

Facing the threat and aggression on the part of Western colonialists, the feudal society of China, which had already been greatly weakened, was undergoing a crisis more serious than it had ever experienced before.

Chapter Two

MODERN PERIOD (1840-1919)

The period of approximately 80 years from 1840 when the Opium War began to 1919 when the May Fourth Movement started was the modern period of China. During this period, the Qing Dynasty ended and the Republic of China began. It was a period when imperialism from abroad and feudalism at home combined to reduce China to a semi-colonial and semi-feudal status. It was also a period when the Chinese people waged a heroic struggle against the imperialists and their running dogs in China. It was a period of democratic revolution led by the bourgeoisie. After 1919, the leadership of the democratic revolution was taken over by the proletariat and its political party. We call the period before 1919 the period of old-democratic revolution and the period after 1919 the period of new-democratic revolution.

1. OPIUM WAR AND TAIPING HEAVENLY KINGDOM

Opium Ban. Before the fourth decade of the 19th century, Britain was the most developed capitalist country in the world. Having strengthened its control over India, it immediately targeted China as its next object of aggression. Then China was a feudal isolationist society, with a combination of small-scale agriculture and domestic handicraft industry as the dominant mode of production. Among the peasants, men tilled and women wove, and they produced most of what they needed in terms of food, clothing, and other daily necessities. Cotton textiles and woollens produced in Britain were not well received in China. As a result, British capitalists must ship a huge amount of silver to China in exchange for tea, silk, and other products.

To rob China of its wealth, the British capitalists resorted to armed smuggling and bribery of Chinese officials who then allowed them to ship large quantities of opium to China. In 1820, the amount of opium shipped to China was 4,000 chests (each chest weighed approximately 133 lbs.); it increased to 40,000 chests in 1838. During the 20 years before 1840, the outflow of silver from China was as much as 100 million taels. The price of silver increased, the burden to the peasants became heavier and heavier, and the Qing government also experienced greater and greater financial difficulties. Meanwhile, the number of opium smokers increased by leaps and bounds, the feudal rulers of China became more and more corrupt, and the fighting capacity of the Chinese army deteriorated steadily. Emperor Daoguang was afraid that his own position as ruler of China might be adversely affected. In 1838, he sent Lin Zexu as imperial commissioner to Guangzhou, with the special mission of banning the opium traffic.

Lin Zexu arrived at Guangzhou in March 1839 and ordered all the opium merchants to hand over their holdings. Charles Elliot, the British superintendent of trade in China, was forced to hand over more than 20,000 chests of opium, weighing as much as 1.15 million kilogrammes. Approximately 1,500 of the 20,000 chests belonged to

American merchants. On June 3, Lin Zexu ordered all this confiscated opium to be publicly burned at the Humen beach. Having destroyed the opium, he ordered that trade between China and Britain be restored, but under no circumstances would the British merchants be allowed to bring in any more opium.

In June 1840, Britain, in the name of protecting its merchants, dispatched more than 40 ships and 4,000 men to attack the coastal areas of Guangdong. Thus the Opium War began. Noticing that the people in Guangzhou had been well prepared in defence, the invaders moved to attack Xiamen, Fujian Province, where they were likewise repulsed. Later, they attacked and captured Dinghai, Zhejiang Province, and continued to move northward. In August, they reached the Tianjin area. Under the threat of big guns, the Qing government began to waver. It relieved Lin Zexu of his duties and ordered him to be investigated and punished. It sent a leading capitulationist named Qishan to Guangzhou to negotiate peace with the British army.

In January 1841, Qishan signed the draft Convention of Chuanbi with the British, whereby China ceded Hongkong to Britain and opened Guangzhou as a trading port. Emperor Daoguang, regarding the cession of territories and the payment of indemnities as an insult to the imperial authority, declared war on Britain and appointed his nephew Yishan to be in charge of military affairs in Guangzhou. In February, the British once again attacked Humen, and the 400 Chinese defenders, under the leadership of a patriot named Guan Tianpei, fought to the last drop of their blood. In May, the British bombarded Guangzhou with artillery fire, and Yishan raised white flags and surrendered. Upon reaching Sanyuanli, a vil-

lage in the northern suburb of Guangzhou, British soldiers began their customary pillage. Angered, the vil-
lagers, assisted by peasants from 103 other villages,
fought back and killed and wounded many British soldiers.

Upon receiving the draft Convention of Chuanbi, the
British government was unhappy with its terms which,
it believed, were too lenient towards the Chinese. Instead of ratifying the treaty, it ordered Henry Pottinger,
at the head of 26 ships and 3,500 men, to enlarge the war
of aggression. The invaders captured Xiamen in August
and Dinghai in October. China also lost Zhenhai and
Ningbo. In June 1842, the British attacked Wusong at
the mouth of the Changjiang River, and then captured
Shanghai and Zhejiang. In August, British warships
appeared on the Changjiang River outside of Nanjing.
The Qing government then sent an imperial commissioner named Qiying to a British warship to sign the humiliating document known as the Sino-British Treaty of
Nanjing.

Sino-British Treaty of Nanjing. This treaty, consisting of 13 articles, was the first unequal treaty that
China signed with a foreign aggressor. Principally, it
stipulated that China open five ports (Guangzhou, Fuzhou, Xiamen, Ningbo, and Shanghai) for trade, cede
Hongkong to the British, and pay an indemnity of 21
million silver dollars. It also stipulated that the tariff
on British goods be subject to negotiations between the
two countries.

The very next year, the British forced the Qing
government to sign two more documents supplementary
to the Treaty of Nanjing. They were the "General Reg-
ulations Governing Anglo-Chinese Trade in the Five

Trading Ports of Guangzhou, Xiamen, Fuzhou, Ningbo, and Shanghai", and the Sino-British Treaty of Humen. The two documents stipulated that Chinese tariff on British goods be limited to 5 per cent, and that the British be given the right to rent land and build houses in the five ports. The latter provision paved the way for the so-called "concessions" in the trading ports. Besides, the British acquired the right of consular jurisdiction and the most-favoured-nation treatment.

In 1844, the United States and France forced the Qing government to sign the Sino-American Treaty of Wangxia and the Sino-French Treaty of Huangpu, respectively. Through these two treaties, the United States and France acquired all the privileges provided in the Treaty of Nanjing and its supplementary documents, with the exception of the cession of territories and the payment of indemnities. In addition, the Americans also gained the special privilege of sending warships to Chinese ports "for the protection of the commerce of their country", and of building churches and hospitals in the five ports of trade. Meanwhile, the French had succeeded in forcing the Chinese government to lift the ban against missionary activities on the part of Roman Catholics who, from then on, could propagate their faith as they wished. The Protestant missionaries soon gained the same privilege.

The signing of the Treaty of Nanjing and other unequal treaties meant that China had lost its rights as a sovereign nation. The inflow of foreign goods into China without restriction caused the slow but sure disintegration of the feudal economy. Step by step China was transformed into a semi-colonial and semi-feudal society. The contradiction between the Chinese nation and foreign capitalists slowly rose to become the principal contradiction. From then on, the revolutionary movement in China had a dual goal: it opposed capitalist aggressors from abroad as it fought feudal rulers at home.

Jintian Uprising. After the Opium War, the suffering of the Chinese people intensified, as they were subject to the dual oppression by foreign capitalists and domestic feudalists. Between 1841 and 1850, more than 100 peasant uprisings were recorded. In 1851, the numerous streams of people's resistance merged to form a gigantic torrent, which was none other than the Taiping Uprising led by Hong Xiuquan.

Hong Xiuquan (1814-64), a native of Huaxian, Guangdong Province, was born to a peasant family. He was, at one time, a village teacher. Around the time of the Opium War, he personally witnessed the cruelty of foreign aggressors, the corruption and decadence of the Qing government, and the poverty and misery of the Chinese peasants. Gradually, he cultivated the thought of revolt. In 1843, he, improving upon some of the Christian ideas, organized a secret society and called it Society of God Worshippers. Among its first members were his schoolmate Feng Yunshan and his cousin Hong Rengan.

In 1844, Hong Xiuquan and Feng Yunshan went to Guiping, Guangxi, where they propagated the new faith among the poverty-stricken peasants. Shortly afterwards, Hong returned to Huaxian, where he wrote such pamphlets as *Doctrines on Salvation*. It was then that he proposed that "all people belong to one family and should share and enjoy the universal peace". This meant equality of all people, regardless of their political and economic status, sex, or nationality.

On January 11, 1851, Hong Xiuquan formally raised

the standard of revolt in the village of Jintian, Guiping, Guangxi. He called his regime the Taiping (Great Peace) Heavenly Kingdom and his army the Taiping Army, or the Army of Great Peace. In September, the Taiping Army attacked and captured Yongan (Mengshan, modern Guangxi) and introduced a new political and military system. The first stage of the new regime materialized.

In April 1852, the Taiping Army broke through the encirclement at Yongan, passed through Guangxi and Hunan, and attacked Hubei. In January 1853, it captured Wuchang, capital of Hubei Province, and enlarged its ranks to 500,000 men. In February, it abandoned Wuchang and moved eastward along the Changjiang River. The Qing army collapsed without a fight. In March, the Taiping Army attacked and captured Nanjing. Nanjing was renamed Tianjing or Heavenly Capital, and made capital of the new regime.

Then the Taiping Heavenly Kingdom made public "The Land System of the Heavenly Kingdom", which contained the idea, "All land under Heaven must be tilled by all the people under Heaven". Land was to be distributed according to household membership, regardless of sex, and each person would receive both good and bad land. A measure of this kind reflected the demand of the peasants for the abolition of the feudal landownership, but it also reflected the utopian ideal of equalitarianism among small producers, which simply could not be realized.

Northern and Western Expeditions of Taiping Army. In May 1853, more than 20,000 men of the Taiping Army moved northward and went as far as Tianjin. The single contingent, having penetrated deep into the enemy's territory, suffered defeat after two years of bloody fighting.

Simultaneously, another contingent, consisting of 1,000 ships, moved upward along the Changjiang River to launch a western expedition. The purpose was to capture Anqing, Jiujiang, Wuhan, and other strategic cities so as to control the upper reaches of the river, protect Tianjing, and enlarge the new regime's territory. Bureaucrats and landlords began to organize their own counter-revolutionary forces for the purpose of suppressing the Taipings. The most cruel and bitter enemy of the Taiping regime proved to be Zeng Guofan (1811-72), head of the Hunan Army. In Hubei, Hunan, Jiangxi, and Anhui, the Taiping Army repeatedly defeated the Hunan Army and won control of eastern Hubei and most of Jiangxi and Anhui after three years of see-saw battle.

After the Taiping regime had located its capital at Nanjing, the Qing government retaliated by organizing the Great South Camp and the Great North Camp outside Nanjing and Yangzhou, respectively. The purpose was to control the insurgents' capital by controlling the approaches to it. During the first half of 1856, the Taiping Army succeeded in destroying the two camps, thus eliminating the threat to its capital. This was the time when, militarily, the Taiping regime reached its highest point.

Later Stage of Taiping Heavenly Kingdom. At the time when the new regime's military fortune was at its highest, internal struggle developed openly among its leaders. Wei Changhui, an ambitious man, killed the outstanding military leader Yang Xiuqing and more than 20,000 of his followers. Supported by both military and civil officials in Tianjing, Hong Xiuquan killed Wei Changhui. But another leader named Shi Dakai, mistrusted by Hong Xiuquan, left the capital with more than

100,000 men and fought alone. In 1863, his army was surrounded by the Qing army on the bank of the Dadu River in Sichuan and was completely wiped out.

The fortune of the Heavenly Kingdom deteriorated fast on account of the internal struggle among its leaders. The Qing army seized the opportunity and counter-attacked; it recovered many places in the middle and lower valleys of the Changjiang and reinstalled the Great North and the Great South Camps. Once again, it surrounded Tianjing on all sides. The military fortune of the Heavenly Kingdom went downward, from offensive and victory to defence and resistance.

To turn the tables on the enemy, Hong Xiuquan promoted two young generals, Chen Yucheng and Li Xiucheng, to be in charge of the military command, and Hong Rengan to be the premier. In 1858, the joint forces of Generals Chen and Li defeated and destroyed the Qing army's Great North Camp and won great victories in the battle of Sanhezhen, Anhui Province. In May 1860, once again the Taiping Army destroyed the Great South Camp and, subsequently, occupied large areas in Jiangsu and Zhejiang provinces. For the time being, the threat to Tianjing was removed. Later, the Hunan Army counter-attacked and surrounded Anqing, an outside shield of Tianjing. In September 1861, Anqing fell; in 1862, Chen Yucheng, then only 26 years old, was captured and executed. The Hunan Army moved eastward along the Changjiang River and pressed hard upon Tianjing.

Second Opium War. The British and French aggressors were rebuffed when they made new demands that the existing treaties with the Qing government be revised at China's expense. Frustrated, they created one incident after another until, in 1857, they had enough excuses to start another war of aggression. Since this war, basically speaking, was an extension and expansion of the Opium War of 1840, it has been referred to as the Second Opium War.

In December 1857, the allied forces of Britain and France attacked and captured Guangzhou and then moved northward along the coast. In May 1858, they occupied Tianjin and then announced that they would soon attack Beijing. Russia and the United States dispatched their envoys to "mediate", but the envoys went along with the allied forces to march north. Hurriedly, the Qing government sent representatives to Tianjin to negotiate peace with the aggressors. In June, Russia, the United States, Britain, and France forced the Qing government to sign with them the Treaties of Tianjin. The major points in these treaties were: that the powers be granted permanent representation in Beijing; that Niuzhuang (later changed to Yingkou), Qiongzhou, Hankou, Jiujiang, Nanjing, Dengzhou (later changed to Yantai), Tainan, Danshui, Chaozhou (later changed to Shantou), and Zhenjiang — all these 10 ports be added as trading ports; that foreigners be allowed to tour, trade and preach their religious beliefs in China's hinterland; that foreign merchant and naval vessels be allowed to ply between the trading ports; and that the Chinese government pay an indemnity of two million taels of silver each to Britain and France. Later, the Qing government was also forced to legitimize opium trade and to employ the British to administer Chinese Maritime Customs.

Under the pretext that the exchange of treaty ratifications had encountered obstructions, Britain and France launched another war of aggression in 1860. The allied forces occupied Tianjin in August, and early in October, they arrived in Beijing where they plundered on a large scale and burned to the ground the world-famous Yuan Ming Yuan Summer Palace. Emperor Xianfeng, who had fled to Rehe, send his younger brother Yixin (Prince Gong) to Beijing to negotiate peace with the invaders. Thus the Sino-British and Sino-French Conventions of Beijing were signed. They provided that the Treaties of Tianjin remain effective; that Tianjin be added as a new port of trade; that Jianshazui (Toconshatsuy) of Kowloon be ceded to Britain; that Britain and France be allowed to recruit Chinese labourers to work in their respective colonies; and that the indemnity paid to Britain and France be increased to eight million taels of silver for each nation. After the Conventions of Beijing were signed, the aggressors withdrew from Beijing, and the Second Opium War ended.

Occupation of Chinese Territories by Tsarist Russia. Beginning in the fourth decade of the 19th century, tsarist Russia continued to violate the eastern sector of the Sino-Russion boundary as stipulated in the Treaty of Nipchu of 1689, as it repeatedly invaded the lower valley of the Heilong River and the Sakhalin Island. When Britain and France launched the Second Opium War and attacked Tianjin, tsarist Russia "pillaged while the Chinese house was on fire". In May 1858, it forced Yishan, then the govenor of Heilongjiang, to sign the Sino-Russian Treaty of Aigun whereby it robbed China of its territories south of the Outer Hinggan Mountains and north of the Heilong River, totalling 600,000 square kilometres. In addition, about 400,000 square kilometres of Chinese territory east of the Wusuli River was defined as "jointly controlled". Subsequently, it forcibly occupied China's

Haishenwei and renamed it Vladivostok. In November
1860, while the allied forces of Britain and France were
pillaging Beijing, tsarist Russia threatened China with
war and forced the Qing government to sign the Sino-
Russian Treaty of Beijing whereby about 400,000 square
kilometres of Chinese territory east of the Wusuli River
was made Russian territory. In addition, by invoking
this treaty and the Sino-Russian Protocol of Chuguchak,
which the Qing government was forced to sign in 1864,
tsarist Russia forcibly took over 440,000 square kilometres of Chinese territory south and east of Lake Balkhash. The total amount of territories seized from China
by tsarist Russia, during and after the Second Opium
War, measured 1.5 million square kilometres. Tsarist
Russia, in fact, was the biggest robber of Chinese territories.

During and after the Second Opium War, China lost
not only more territories but also more sovereignty as a
nation. The aggressive influence of foreign countries
spread from the coast to the interior, and the Qing government, more and more, was subjected to the control by
foreign powers.

**Collusion Between Domestic and Foreign Reac-
tionaries. Failure of the Taipings.** To assist the Qing
government to suppress the Taiping uprising, an American named F. T. Ward organized a so-called "Foreign
Rifle Detachment", and the British and the French also
organized counter-revolutionary armed units: all of them
wanted to end the Taiping regime. But the Taiping
Army's attitude towards foreign aggressors was resolute:
it repeatedly dealt severely with the enemy. It killed,
wounded, or captured alive some foreign commanders,
including the American F. T. Ward, who was killed in

action in Zhejiang. However, the Taiping regime could not persist long when confronted with a coalition of domestic and foreign enemies. In June 1864, Hong Xiuquan died of illness. On July 19, Tianjing (Nanjing) fell into the hands of the enemy. The great peasant movement came to a sad end.

Nevertheless, the peasant movement of Taiping lasted altogether 14 years. The Taipings captured more than 600 cities and extended their influence to 18 provinces. They shook the Qing regime to its foundation, and struck successfully against aggressive forces from abroad. All this aroused and strengthened the revolutionary will of the Chinese people.

2. "WESTERNIZATION" MOVEMENT, SINO-FRENCH WAR AND SINO-JAPANESE WAR

"Westernization" Movement. During the period between the sixth and ninth decades of the 19th century, a number of bureaucrats, in order to maintain their feudal, corrupt rule and continue to oppress the people, adopted technology of the Western capitalist countries and introduced some modern industries. Assisted and supported by foreign aggressors, they even built a new army and navy. All these activities are referred to by historians as the "Westernization" movement. The bureaucrats active in this movement belonged to the so-called "Westernization" group, as differentiated from the diehards in the ruling clique who did not want any change at all. The leaders of the "Westernization" group were Yixin, Zeng Guofan, Li Hongzhang, and Zuo Zongtang. Beginning in the 1860s, the "Westernization" group introduced some modern armament industries. In 1861, Zeng Guofan established in Anqing an ammunition factory. In 1865, Li Hongzhang founded in Shanghai the Jiangnan Arsenal specialized in the manufacturing of rifles, artillery pieces, ammunition, and steamships. In 1866, Zuo Zongtang set up in Fuzhou the Mawei Shipyard for the construction of warships. In 1867, the Qing government established the Tianjin Machinery Factory for the manufacturing of firearms. In addition, there were ammunitions factories of smaller size across the country. In the name of strengthening China, leaders of the "Westernization" group were in fact only interested in using the new equipment to suppress the people, instead of resisting foreign aggression.

From the 1870s to the 1890s, while attempting to develop an armament industry, the leaders of the "Westernization" movement also built some factories for non-military uses. Altogether they numbered about 20. Among the most important were: the China Merchants Steamship Navigation Company (set up in 1872), the Kaiping Coal Mine (1878), the Shanghai Machine Textile Factory (1890), the Hubei Textile Factory (1892), and the Hanyang Ironworks (1893). In 1880, rail was laid between Tangshan and Xugezhuang for the transport of coal; 11 kilometres in length, it was China's first railway. Some of these enterprises were owned and managed by the government; others were enterprises which, run by the merchants under government supervision, or jointly run by the government and merchants, absorbed capital from landlords, bureaucrats, and merchants. In the name of "enriching the nation", the bureaucrats in control of these enterprises were most interested in enriching themselves, instead of developing social production. Yet they were the first people who built modern industries in China. They proposed the adoption of Western technology for production; they, in that sense, did objectively help the development of the social productive forces and the growth of Chinese capitalism.

In the 1880s, Li Hongzhang, governor-general of Zhili and Commissioner for Northern Affairs, founded a naval academy in Tianjin, a dockyard at Lüshun, and a naval port at Weihaiwei. Furthermore, he also bought ships and artillery pieces from foreign countries and established and expanded the Northern Navy. Meanwhile, Zuo Zongtang founded in Mawei, Fujian Province, the Southern Navy.

The "Westernization" group characterized the measures it had adopted as a "new programme", the purpose of which was supposed to enrich and strengthen China through its own effort. However, it did not make China rich or strong. Instead, the country was subjected to even greater control by foreign aggressors, militarily, politically, and economically. Meanwhile, crisis developed in China's border regions, and the Sino-French War and Sino-Japanese War broke out.

Crisis in Border Regions. The competition for colonies and the division of the world into spheres of influence among the capitalist countries reached a high point after the 1870s. Some countries bordering on China were reduced to colonies one after another, and crisis developed in China's border regions.

In 1865, Yakub Beg, army commander of Khohand in Central Asia (then independent but later absorbed by tsarist Russia), led troops to invade the southern section of China's Xinjiang Province. In 1871, tsarist Russia sent troops to occupy Ili, then capital of Xinjiang, and the

surrounding areas. In 1877, the Qing government decisively defeated Yakub Beg and recovered all the lost territories in southern Xinjiang. In February 1881, tsarist
Russia forced the Qing government to sign with it the
Sino-Russian Treaty of St. Petersburg. Though China
recovered Ili under this treaty, it lost to the Russians the
vast area west of the Khorgos River. Invoking this treaty
and other documents signed between 1882 and 1884 relating to the delimitation of Sino-Russian boundaries, the
Russians annexed more than 70,000 square kilometres of
additional Chinese territories in Xinjiang. In 1892,
tsarist Russia sent troops to occupy another 20,000 square
kilometres of Chinese territories located to the west of
the Sarykol Mountains in the Pamirs region.

While slowly taking over Burma, Britain extended
its aggressive influence towards China's southwestern
borders. In 1876, it compelled the Qing government to
sign the Sino-British Agreement of Yantai which facilitated its aggressive activities in Yunnan, Tibet, Sichuan,
Qinghai, and Gansu. In 1888, it launched an aggressive
war against Tibet. Later, it forced the Qing government
to conclude with it an unequal treaty whereby Yadong in
Tibet was designated as a trading port. From then on,
the British, using India and Burma as the base of operation, continued their aggression against Yunnan and
Tibet.

Sino-French War. While busy with its aggression
against Viet Nam, France attempted to invade China's
Yunnan Province by way of that country. Intensified
French aggression eventually led to the Sino-French War
of 1884-85. The Black Flag Army, a peasant rebel force
led by Liu Yongfu, struck repeatedly against the French
aggressors. In March 1885, a Chinese general named

Feng Zicai decisively defeated the French aggressors at
the Zhennan Pass (known as Friendship Pass today), a
defeat which caused the then French cabinet to collapse.
But the corrupt Qing government, announcing that it
would "end the war while victorious", sent Li Hongzhang
to Tianjin to sign with France a humiliating treaty. Thus
"China was defeated while victorious, and France was
victorious while defeated". The treaty opened new
ports for trade in the border areas between Viet Nam
and China's Yunnan and Guangxi provinces. It also
compelled the Chinese to hire Frenchmen in railway
building. The door to China's southwest was now wide
open.

Sino-Japanese War and Treaty of Shimonoseki.
Japan's ambition of occupying Korea and then invading
the Chinese mainland was not new. In the spring of
1894, a peasant uprising led by the Tonghak ("Eastern
Learning") Society occurred in Korea, and the feudal
Korean government requested assistance from China to
suppress the uprising. Early in June, Chinese troops
arrived at Asan, Korea. Japan also sent troops to Korea,
captured the Korean king, and occupied the Korean city
Seoul. It then challenged the Chinese presence, leading
to the Sino-Japanese War.

There was no question about the bravery of the rank
and file among China's military after the war began.
Army officer Zuo Baogui and navy officer Deng Shichang,
together with the men they led, fought heroically and
brilliantly against the enemy until they were killed in
action. But the capitulationists, led by Empress Dowager
Cixi and Li Hongzhang, had no preparation for the war
at all; they, instead, relied heavily on the intervention by
Russia and Britain to stop Japan's advance. Their in-

fluence was extensive, and they sped up China's defeat. Japan occupied not only Korea but also the Liaodong Peninsula and Weihaiwei.

In 1895, Japan forced the Qing government to sign the humiliating Treaty of Shimonoseki. The treaty provided, among other things, that the Qing government cede to Japan the Liaodong Peninsula and Taiwan together with the adjacent islands and the Penghu Islands; that China pay Japan an indemnity of 200 million taels of silver; that Shashi, Chongqing, Suzhou, and Hangzhou be added as trading ports; that Japan be allowed to establish in the trading ports consular offices and factories and to ship to China machinery of all kinds.

Tsarist Russia's ambition to occupy China's northeast was not new either. After China signed the Treaty of Shimonoseki with Japan, tsarist Russia, together with France and Germany, brought pressure to bear on Japan and successfully forced the latter to return the Liaodong Peninsula to China. China, in turn, paid an additional indemnity of 30 million taels of silver. Two years later, tsarist Russia itself sent troops to occupy Lüshun and Dalian, both of which are located on the Liaodong Peninsula.

After the signing of the Treaty of Shimonoseki, the ambition of the powers to partition China was whipped up. The payment of large indemnities meant that China, from then on, must borrow regularly from foreign countries. Its reliance on the imperialists became greater, and the burden on the Chinese people became heavier. After China had granted Japan the privilege to open factories in China, other imperialist powers, by invoking the most-favoured-nation clause, wanted to receive and did receive the same. All this not only enabled the imperialists to export capital to China and rob it of its wealth but also dealt a severe blow to the development of China's national industries. The Treaty of Shimonoseki was the most damaging to the Chinese interest among all the unequal treaties after the Treaty of Nanjing. It sped up China's downward rush to a semi-colonial status.

Taiwan was an integral part of China dating back to ancient times. The people in Taiwan were furious when they heard that their province had been ceded to Japan. Under the leadership of Liu Yongfu, who was now in charge of the defence of Taiwan, they organized themselves as volunteers and fought against the invaders from Japan. In less than five months, they exterminated more than 32,000 of the invaders. But the Qing government subjected the island to a blockade; Liu Yongfu and the Taiwan people, without outside support, failed in the end. During the subsequent 50 years when Japan occupied Taiwan, the Taiwan people continued to fight against the occupationists and for the return of Taiwan to the motherland.

Imperialist Activities for Partitioning China.   The end of the Sino-Japanese War in 1895 marked the beginning of competition among the imperialist powers to export capital to China. Then the total revenue of the Qing government was about 80 million taels of silver per year, which could not even meet the yearly expenditures. Now that there was an additional outlay for the payment of indemnities, the imperialist powers competed among themselves to lend money to China. The British minister went as far as saying that his country would have to resort to the use of armed forces if China did not borrow from it. In the five years after the conclusion of the Sino-Japanese War, the Qing government borrowed from Britain, Russia, France and Germany a total of 370 million taels of silver. All these loans were secured on the receipts of China's Maritime Customs. Through these loans, the imperialists not only earned high interest but also controlled China's finance. Besides, they established in China banks, through which they could export more capital to the country, issue paper currency, and further manipulate Chinese finance. Having obtained the rights to invest and open factories in China, they, in the five years between 1895 and 1900, established 933 factories on Chinese soil. They occupied a dominant position in such activities as railway construction, river navigation, and mining. Meanwhile, they were busy with the creation of "concessions" and "spheres of influence". They were rising high on the wave of partitioning China.

In November 1897, Germany forced China to lease to it the Jiaozhou Bay, the lease being supposed to last 99 years. It also obtained the right to build a railway from Jiaozhou to Jinan and the right to mine minerals within 15 kilometres of both sides of the railway. From then on, Shandong became a German sphere of influence.

In June 1896, Li Hongzhang signed with tsarist Russia a secret treaty which provided that tsarist Russia had the right to build, in the two provinces of Heilongjiang and Jilin, the Chinese Eastern Railway which would link the Trans-Siberian Railway with Vladivostok by a direct route. In September, through a contract on the Chinese Eastern Railway, tsarist Russia acquired the right of administering areas adjacent to the railway and the rights of transporting troops, opening mines and using the land free of charge, along the railway. In December 1897, it dispatched warships to Lüshun and Dalian and occupied them by force. In March 1898, it forced the

Qing government to lease Lüshun to it as a naval base
and Dalian as a commercial port. Besides, tsarist Russia
obtained the right to build a branch railway that would
link Harbin with Dalian. Thus all of China's northeast
became a Russian sphere of influence.

In 1897, France forced the Qing government to promise that China would never cede the Hainan Island and
the land opposite to it across the sea to any foreign country other than France. In 1898, China was compelled to
lease to France the Guangzhou Bay. In addition, France
obtained from the Qing government the right to build
railways and open mines in the provinces of Yunnan and
Guangxi. It also made the Qing government promise that
China would not cede the provinces of Yunnan, Guangxi,
and Guangdong to any foreign country other than France.
Thus the three provinces became a French sphere of influence.

The aggressive influence of Britain had been in the
Changjiang valley for a long time. In 1898, as a counter-
balance to tsarist Russia's occupation of Lüshun and Dalian, Britain dispatched troops to occupy Weihaiwei which
was later leased to it. In view of France's increasing influence in south China, Britain forced the Qing government to lease to it the Kowloon Peninsula, the islands adjacent to Hongkong, and the bays of Dapeng and Shen-
zhen. It also made the Qing government promise and
declare publicly that under no circumstances would China cede the provinces along the Changjiang River and the
provinces of Guangdong and Yunnan to any foreign
country other than Britain. Thus the Changjiang valley
became a British sphere of influence, and the provinces
of Guangdong and Yunnan became a joint sphere of influence of Britain and France.

Also in 1898, under the pretext that the province of Fujian was located next to Taiwan, Japan forced the Qing government to declare that China would not cede or lease Fujian to any foreign country other than Japan. Thus the province of Fujian became a Japanese sphere of influence.

During the three years between 1896 and 1899, the principal areas in China were divided up among the imperialist powers as spheres of influence. All the important ports of China became leased territories where foreign countries anchored their warships. The right to construct major railways and to open major mines had fallen, or began to fall, into foreign hands.

At the end of the American-Spanish War, the division of China into spheres of influence had already become a *fait accompli*. In 1899, the United States proposed to Britain, Russia, Germany, Japan, Italy, and France the so-called "open door" policy, which these countries later accepted. Using the pretext of equal opportunity and joint sharing of benefits, the United States demanded that China open its door to Americans, too, so that they could operate in the foreign spheres of influence in China and share equal benefits. From then on, U.S. aggression against China was conducted on a larger and larger scale.

3. BOURGEOIS REFORM MOVEMENT AND YIHETUAN MOVEMENT

Chinese Proletariat in Its Early Days and Emergence of National Bourgeoisie. Long before the Opium War, Chinese capitalism had begun to develop. Foreign capitalism entered China after the Opium War, and this created favourable conditions for its growth. Beginning in the 1870s, a number of merchants, landlords, and bureaucrats founded modern enterprises of their own. Early in the 1890s, enterprises of this kind numbered more than 100, employing nearly 30,000 workers. They concentrated on light industries such as silk reeling, cotton textiles, flour milling, paper making, printing, and match manufacturing, though there were also some mining enterprises. Generally speaking, these enterprises were small in scale. With the appearance of national enterprises, the national bourgeoisie emerged. But the proletariat arrived earlier than the national bourgeoisie.

Beginning in the 1840s, Britain, France, and some other countries illegally established in the trading ports shipyards and factories that hired Chinese workers. These workers were in fact China's first industrial workers. The factories set up by the "Westernization" group since the 1860s also employed industrial workers. Since the 1870s, as national capitalism appeared and grew, the ranks of China's industrial workers expanded. That is why the Chinese proletariat is older and more experienced than China's national bourgeoisie.

Background of the Reform Movement. After the Sino-Japanese War, many Chinese cried aloud about the necessity of building China's own industry ("Establish factories for national salvation"), as foreign capital kept on coming in and as the "Westernization" movement was bankrupt and totally discredited. Between 1895 and 1898, private enterprises newly set up in such areas as textiles, silk reeling, flour milling, navigation, and coal mining numbered as many as 62, with a total investment of as much as 12.4 million silver dollars, which exceeded the accumulated investment during the 30 years prior to the Sino-

Japanese War. As its influence increased, the national
bourgeoisie demanded further development of national
industry and commerce; it also demanded a share of political power. It, naturally, wanted the Qing government
to carry out some much-needed reforms that would be
beneficial to the development of capitalism.

As early as the seventh and eighth decades of the
19th century, a number of intellectuals, influenced by
bourgeois ideas and having witnessed the intensity of
foreign aggression and the inability of a corrupt government to cope with it, advocated reforms. Their representatives were Feng Guifen, Wang Tao, Zheng Guanying,
and Ma Jianzhong. They wrote books, spoke on current affairs, and proposed reforms which, according to
them, would make China strong. In the 1890s when the
problem of national salvation became even more serious,
the thought of reform slowly acquired a new meaning
and became a political movement with the support of the
masses. Kang Youwei (1858-1927), Liang Qichao (1873-
1929), Tan Sitong (1865-98), and Yan Fu (1853-1921) were
representatives of this line of thinking. They believed
that the salvation of the country depended upon the conduct of reforms and that China must learn from the capitalist countries of the West if the reforms were to be
successful. Learning from the West meant not only the
learning of its science and technology but also its political
institutions. They, therefore, advocated the adoption of
constitutional monarchy. When the sad news of the
signing of the Treaty of Shimonoseki (1895) arrived, Kang
Youwei was in Beijing taking the metropolitan examination. He sent Emperor Guangxu a petition, that bore
the signatures of 1,300 examination candidates, to indicate his opposition to the treaty. He requested the

conduct of reforms. From 1888 to 1898, altogether he presented seven petitions to Emperor Guangxu requesting the same. Intellectuals like him published newspapers, opened schools, and organized academic societies, all for the purpose of impressing the public on the seriousness of the national crisis and on the importance of conducting reforms.

Reform and Defeat. Prior to the Sino-Japanese War, controversies developed among the Qing rulers. On the one side was the faction headed by Emperor Guangxu; on the other side was the faction headed by Empress Dowager Cixi. Emperor Guangxu (1871-1908) ascended the throne in 1875 at the age of four. He was supposed to have taken over the reins of government in 1887, but real power remained in the hands of Empress Dowager Cixi. When the nation was in serious danger following the Sino-Japanese War, the emperor's faction wanted to conduct reforms in order to take power away from the empress dowager's faction, and the reformists themselves wished to rely on the emperor's support to transform their dream into reality.

The occupation of the Jiaozhou Bay by Germany in November 1897 signalled that the partition of China was imminent. The very next year Kang Youwei stated, in a petition to Emperor Guangxu, that China must conduct reforms to forestall the impending disaster. The emperor accepted the petitioner's proposal and appointed some of the reformists to be court officials. From June 11 to September 21, 1898, a series of imperial decrees were issued to authorize the reforms. Economically, there would be in the central government a bureau of agriculture, industry, and commerce to promote development in these fields. There would be a bureau respon-

sible for the construction of railways and the opening
of mines. Reforms would also be introduced in the administration of the nation's finance, and a budgetary
system would be adopted. Politically, citizens would be
allowed to publish their own newspapers and to petition
to the emperor on current affairs. Laws would be rec-
tified, surplus personnel in government be dismissed, and
the government be made honest and incorruptible; new
methods would be adopted for the training of the army
and the navy. Culturally, the examination system would
be revised, the stereotyped "eight-legged" essays be abolished, and scientific works and inventions be encouraged.
All the private academies, family shrines and temples
would be converted into elementary and middle schools.
In the capital of Beijing there would be an imperial college (which proved to be the forerunner of Beijing University), and both Western and Chinese subjects would be
taught in all schools. There would be a translation
bureau to render foreign works into Chinese.

Emperor Guangxu's reforms were directed from
above; they were not meant to change the feudal structure since it would be kept intact. But the diehards, led
by Cixi, regarded them as "flood and beasts" and stated
openly that it was better to let the nation die than to conduct any kind of reforms. They used all their might to
obstruct and to make sure that the reforms would not
succeed. Besides, the reforms had no basis of mass support, and they remained empty words. On September
21, 1898, Cixi, with the support of Ronglu and Yuan Shikai (1858-1916), staged a coup and ordered the imprison-
ment of Emperor Guangxu, whereupon she openly took
the reins of government into her own hands. With the
exception of the Imperial College in Beijing which was

allowed to continue to function, all the reform measures were abolished. Having been informed of the coup in advance, Kang Youwei and Liang Qichao fled to foreign countries, but six other leading reformists including Tan Sitong were arrested and killed. From the beginning to the end, the reform lasted 103 days; that is why it has often been referred to as "Hundred Days' Reform".

Since the purpose of this reform was to change the status quo and rescue the country from its impending peril, besides the development of capitalism, it was a progressive movement at that time.

Peasants' Yihetuan Movement. The prospect of China's partition among the imperialist powers remained after the failure of the "Hundred Days' Reform". In response, the labouring masses took up arms and launched a patriotic, anti-imperialist movement of their own. The movement was known as Yihetuan (Society of Righteousness and Harmony).

It was not accidental that the Yihetuan began in Shandong, since Shandong was the province that suffered much from the Japanese aggressors during the Sino-Japanese War. Later, Germany forcibly took over the Jiaozhou Bay and started to build the Jiaozhou Jinan Railway. While building the railway, the Germans tore down houses, forcibly occupied cultivated fields, destroyed water routes, and plundered the mineral resources along the line. Britain, after forcing the Qing government to lease Weihaiwei to it, enclosed two neighbouring counties as its own. All this, plus the dumping of foreign goods in the Chinese market, left many peasants and handicraftsmen jobless and homeless. Even religion was employed as a tool of aggression by the imperialist powers. Towards the end of the 19th century, the num-

ber of foreign missionaries in China, including both the
Catholic and the Eastern Orthodox missionaries, was more
than 3,300, and the number of Chinese converts exceeded
800,000.   In the province of Shandong alone, there were
more than 1,000 Christian churches with more than 80,000
converts.   The missionaries, in collusion with local bullies and other scoundrels, forcibly took over people's properties, collected rent, and engaged in usury.   They often
resorted to violence and killed people at will.   Whenever
there was a dispute, local officials always sided with
them.   Under the circumstances, it was not surprising
that the anti-missionary sentiment became stronger and
stronger with the passage of time.   In 1899, the Yihetuan
Movement exploded in the province of Shandong.

     Yihetuan was originally a secret organization where-
by peasants in Shandong and Zhili (Hebei) resorted to
religion in their anti-Qing struggle.   It used the means
of martial arts and the training it provided to organize
the masses for armed struggle against the reactionaries.
As the imperialists intensified their aggression against
China, they quickly became the target of Yihetuan's re-
sentment and struggle.   In 1899, the once secret organization went public.   Its members burned churches,
chased out the missionaries, and severely punished corrupt
officials and local bullies.   They repeatedly defeated the
Qing army that was sent to suppress them.   As their
strength increased rapidly, the Qing government sent
Yuan Shikai to Shandong to crush them.   In 1900, the
main forces of the Yihetuan were shifted to Zhili where
they joined forces with local groups.   Very quickly, they
moved towards Tianjin and Beijing.   In the summer of
that year, they won control of the nation's capital, Beijing.
Meanwhile, the movement had spread to Shanxi, Henan,

Inner Mongolia, and northeast China as well as south China. This anti-imperialist struggle quickly became nationwide.

Aggression by Eight Allied Powers. As the Yihetuan struck against the imperialists without mercy, eight imperialist countries — Russia, Britain, Germany, France, the United States, Japan, Italy, and Austria — formed an alliance to launch an aggressive war against China. On June 10, 1900, 2,000 of the allied forces, led by a British navy commander named E. H. Seymour, landed on Dagukou and moved towards Tianjin and Beijing. More troops were thrown in later. The heroic Yihetuan quickly engaged the aggressors in bloody combat. But, attacked by reactionaries at home and from abroad, the Yihetuan suffered heavy casualties. On July 14, the allied forces captured Tianjin. On August 4, they, now nearly 20,000 men in strength, proceeded from Tianjin to attack Beijing which they occupied on August 14. For three days, they pillaged the city. All the treasures, documents, and historical relics in the Imperial Palace and in the Summer Palace were looted or otherwise destroyed. Besides, they raped women and put the whole city to fire and sword.

Greatly alarmed by the rapid development of the Yihetuan Movement, the Qing government decided to use the movement's anti-missionary policy to seize popular leadership. It, therefore, declared that the movement was legal. After the allied troops had entered Beijing, the Qing government, headed by Cixi, fled to Xi'an; it then did a complete about-face, declaring that members of the Yihetuan were "rioters". It expressed "friendship" for the foreign invaders and requested them to exterminate the "rioters". Attacked by the bloody hands from both the Qing government and the allied troops, the Yihetuan Movement failed in the end. But the movement itself demonstrated beyond any doubt the enormous strength of the peasant masses in opposing imperialism. It dealt a severe blow to the imperialists who wanted to partition China among themselves. It struck hard against the feudal rule of the Qing government and sped up the early demise of this corrupt regime.

In 1900, tsarist Russia, besides participating in the invasion of the Beijing-Tianjin area together with the seven other nations, also unilaterally dispatched more than 100,000 men to invade the three provinces of China's northeast. Wherever they went, the Russians burned, killed, and pillaged. Not until April 1902 was tsarist Russia forced to agree to withdraw its troops from Chinese territories by stages.

On September 7, 1901, the Qing government signed a treaty of peace with 11 countries (Britain, the United States, Russia, Germany, Austria, France, Italy and Japan, plus Belgium, Spain, and Holland) whereby China was forced to pay an indemnity of 450 million taels of silver in 39 years. Since the unpaid balance carried an annual interest of 4 per cent, total payment amounted to 980 million taels. The treaty also provided that the area of Dongjiaominxiang in Beijing be designated a "legation quarter" where foreign troops would be allowed to station permanently for the protection of foreign embassies; that the Qing government be made responsible for the suppression of the Chinese people's anti-imperialist movement; that the fort at Dagu be dismantled and destroyed; and that the allied nations be allowed to station troops in 12 strategic points along the railway between Beijing and Shanhaiguan. The treaty was the Qing government's biggest sellout, politically, militarily, and economically. From then on, it became a docile agent of the imperialists for their control of China.

4. BOURGEOIS REVOLUTION OF 1911 AND STRUGGLE AGAINST NORTHERN WARLORDS

Sun Yat-sen's Early Revolutionary Activities. After signing the humiliating treaty of 1901, China was subjected to even greater control and plunder by the imperialist powers. Both national and class contradictions sharpened as a result. The anti-imperialist and anti-feudal movement raged like a prairie fire across the country, giving rise to the bourgeois democratic revolution.

Sun Yat-sen (1866-1925) was an originator and leader of China's bourgeois democratic revolution. He was born to a peasant family in Cuiheng Village, Xiangshan County (known as Zhongshan County today), Guangdong Province. During the 14 years between 1878 and 1892, while studying in Honolulu and Hongkong, he was brought into contact with the social and political theories of the bourgeoisie. In 1892, after he had graduated from a medical school in Hongkong, he went to Macao and Guangzhou to propagate revolutionary thought and to participate in political activity, even though, outwardly, he was merely a physician. In the fall of 1894, he once again went to Honolulu where he organized the China Revival Society which proved to be the earliest revolutionary organization of the Chinese bourgeoisie. Early in 1895, he established in Hongkong the headquarters of that society and actively planned for an armed uprising in Guangzhou. In October, the plan was discovered, and the scheduled uprising was aborted before it could take place. Sun Yat-sen was forced to seek refugee in foreign countries. But he continued to spread revolutionary ideas and develop his organization in preparation for another armed uprising.

Spread of Bourgeois Revolutionary Ideas and Establishment of Revolutionary Organizations. Early in the 20th century, new schools were established across the country, and the number of students who went to study in foreign countries also increased enormously. In 1905, the number of Chinese students in Japan alone was 3,200, not to mention those who had gone to study in Europe and America. The revolutionary elements among them wrote books and articles to propagate ideas of a bourgeois democratic revolution. There was a man named Zhang Binglin (or Zhang Taiyan, 1869-1936) who refuted the idea advanced by the reformists Kang Youwei, Liang Qichao, etc. that "China needs a constitutional monarchy, not a revolution". There was another man named Zou Rong (1885-1905) who wrote a book advocating the overthrow of the Qing Dynasty and the establishment of a "Republic of China", and opposing interference of Chinese affairs by foreign powers. His book was reprinted 20 times, and nearly one million copies were sold; it exercised a great influence over the revolutionaries of his time. Finally, there was a man named Chen Tianhua (1875-1905) who had at one time studied in Japan. His works, written in rhymes, exposed the crimes which foreign aggressors had committed against China, pointed out that the Qing government was "a government for foreigners", and called upon the masses to rise in revolution.

Simultaneously with the spreading of revolutionary

ideas, these intellectuals founded revolutionary organizations for concrete action. In November 1903, Huang Xing, Chen Tianhua, and others founded in Changsha the Society for Revival of the Chinese Nation. In the same year, Cai Yuanpei, Zhang Taiyan, and others established in Shanghai the Restoration Society. Both societies had organized armed uprisings, but they did not succeed. In 1905, Liu Jingan and others recruited students and junior officers and soldiers of the New Army and organized the Daily Knowledge Society in Hubei. Like Sun Yat-sen's China Revival Society, all these organizations had a common goal, namely, the overthrow of the Qing government by revolutionary violence.

Birth of China Revolutionary League, and Revolutionary Development. In July 1905, Sun Yat-sen left Europe for Japan. Under his leadership, more than 70 representatives of the China Revival Society, the Society for Revival of the Chinese Nation, the Restoration Society, and the Daily Knowledge Society gathered in Tokyo for the founding of a new organization called China Revolutionary League. The political programme of the new organization, as proposed by Sun Yat-sen, had four points: repulsion of the Manchus, restoration of China, establishment of a republic, and equal landownership. In August, a meeting in Tokyo marked its formal inauguration, and to this meeting came more than 100 delegates from 17 of China's provinces. The meeting passed the new organization's constitution, elected Sun Yat-sen as its director-general, and decided the leadership structure. Later, in an editorial that appeared in the first issue of *People's Journal*, the party organ, Sun Yat-sen developed further his thinking and called the developed idea the Three People's Principles, namely, the Principle of Nationalism, the Principle of Democracy, and the Principle of People's Livelihood. These three principles formed the ideological guide for the revolution he led.

The China Revolutionary League was the first united revolutionary party of the bourgeoisie that was nation-wide in scope. The establishment of this organization and the defining of the Three People's Principles had an important inspiring effect on the revolution's develop-ment. However, there was no ideological and organiza-tional unity in the league, for it remained a loose alliance of the bourgeois and petty-bourgeois revolutionaries and the anti-Manchu landlords. Its programme contained serious shortcomings. It did not say anything about the overthrow of the imperialists; in fact, the league even dreamed of winning the support of the imperialists by recognizing the legitimacy of the unequal treaties and promising to pay the indemnities as stipulated. Even its anti-feudalism was not thorough enough.

After the China Revolutionary League had been es-tablished, secret branches came into being across China and abroad. In less than one year, its membership ex-ceeded 10,000. Its members published more than 100 newspapers and magazines, and its revolutionary ideas spread far and wide.

While spreading and promoting revolutionary ideas, the league launched several armed uprisings. It failed in each and every case, since each uprising was simply a military adventure, and it did not mobilize the masses for support. On April 27, 1911, it launched an armed uprising on a large scale in Guangzhou, and the revolu-tionaries fought for a long day before they, too, failed. Many perished. Later, 72 bodies were found and subse-quently buried in Huanghuagang, Guangzhou. They are

referred to as the Seventy-Two Martyrs of Huanghuagang.

**Wuchang Uprising and Establishment of the Repub-
lic.** During the time when the China Revolutionary
League was active in staging uprisings, people in various
parts of the country launched their own struggles spon-
taneously. The struggles numbered 113 in 1909 and increased to 285 in 1910. In 1911, after the Qing government had sold the rights to build the Guangzhou-Hankou
and Sichuan-Hankou Railways to the imperialists, people
in four provinces — Sichuan, Hunan, Hubei, and Guangdong — staged a mighty protest movement for the protection of railway rights. The struggle was most ferocious in
Sichuan where the insurgents occupied a dozen cities and
county towns. Revolutionaries in other provinces were
also ready for action. The time was ripe for the overthrow
of the Qing Dynasty.

In August 1911, encouraged by the China Revolutionary League, the Literary Association and Society for
Mutual Progress organized by former members of the Daily
Knowledge Society set up a leading organ for an
armed uprising in Wuchang. Then the New Army in
Hubei numbered approximately 15,000 men, one-third of
whom either had close relations with the revolutionary
party or were its secret members. On the evening of
October 10, the armed uprising led by members of the
revolutionary party but staffed mostly by revolutionary
soldiers of the New Army, exploded. A fierce battle went
on throughout the night; by daytime, the insurgents succeeded in taking over the city of Wuchang. Two days
later, they also took Hanyang and Hankou.

The victory of the Wuchang Uprising happily sur-
prised the nation, since people across the country re-

sponsed favourably to it. In less than two months, 15 provinces declared independence from the Qing regime. In December 1911, Sun Yat-sen returned to China from abroad. Towards the end of the month, delegates from the provinces gathered in Nanjing to organize a provisional central government and elected Sun as the provisional president. On New Year's Day, 1912, Sun Yat-sen was sworn in, and the establishment of the Republic of China was formally announced, the year 1912 being marked as its Year One. A provisional national assembly also came into being. In March, Sun Yat-sen promulgated the Provisional Constitution of the Republic of China, which was modelled after the constitution of a bourgeois-democratic republic.

Struggle Against Rule of Northern Warlords. The victory of the Wuchang Uprising dealt a severe blow to the reactionary forces, both at home and abroad. Then the military power of the Qing government was in the hands of Yuan Shikai, head of the Northern warlords, who schemed to wrest the fruits of the revolution. Supported by the imperialists as well as the constitutional monarchists who had wormed their way into the revolutionary camp, he did two things. On the one hand, he forced the last Qing emperor Puyi to abdicate; on the other hand, he, by the use of threat and pressure, made the provisional government in Nanjing hand over power to him and "elect" him the first president of the Republic. The weak-kneed bourgeoisie compromised and retreated. In February 1912, the provisional national assembly in Nanjing, having heard that the last Qing emperor had abdicated, elected Yuan the provisional president. Sun Yat-sen was forced to resign. In March, Yuan Shikai formally assumed the office of the presidency in Beijing. This signalled the failure of the bourgeois revolution. From then on, China was ruled by the Northern warlords.

Yuan Shikai sold China's sovereignty abroad, while cruelly suppressing the people at home. With the support of the imperialists, he even dreamed of becoming an emperor. Though his attempt to restore monarchy to China failed in the end, state power remained in the hands of his successors, namely, other Northern warlords. Whichever clique among these warlords happened to be in control of Beijing, it formed the so-called "central government". Meanwhile, the warlords in the provinces did whatever they pleased, engaging in mutual slaughter. Under the ruthless oppression of imperialism as well as feudalism, the workers, the peasants, and the urban petty bourgeoisie had a difficult time in making a living. The period of the warlord rule was another dark, chaotic period in the history of modern China.

The Chinese people, however, waged a heroic struggle against the reactionary rule of the Northern warlords. In 1915 when Yuan Shikai assumed the imperial title, Yunnan, Guizhou, and Guangxi declared independence and organized an anti-Yuan "Republic Protection Army". This anti-Yuan effort has been referred to by historians as the "Republic Protection Campaign". Condemned by the whole nation, Yuan Shikai relinquished his imperial pretension and died in despair. Duan Qirui, who took over from Yuan in 1916, abolished both the provisional constitution and the parliament. In 1917, Sun Yat-sen called upon the nation to "uphold the constitution and restore the parliament". He went to Guangzhou where he organized an anti-Duan military government for the protection of the constitution. Historians refer to his effort as the "Constitution Protection Campaign". However, devoid of a mass basis and because Sun himself was elbowed aside by the warlords in south China, the campaign failed.

As national capitalism developed, Chinese proletariat grew rapidly. The number of industrial workers was anywhere between 500,000 and 600,000 before 1911, and it increased to two million by 1919. Besides, there were about 12 million handicraftsmen and shop assistants. During this period, the Chinese proletariat had gone on strike for more than 100 times. Their strike struggle showed much progress in terms of scale, the number of participants, the level of the workers' political awareness as well as the degree of organization. In addition to spontaneous struggle for better economic conditions, the workers fought against both the imperialists and the feudal warlords. During the struggle against the Twenty-One Demands which Japan had put to the Northern warlord government and which were aimed at ending China as a sovereign nation, the Chinese proletariat stood and fought on the front line. They were the most resolute contingent among the anti-imperialist, patriotic forces. The increasing strength of the Chinese proletariat laid a solid class foundation for the transition of the Chinese revolution from the old-democratic stage to the new-democratic stage.

5. MODERN CULTURE

Changes in Academic Community. Culture and learning underwent changes after the Opium War. A section of relatively enlightened bureaucrats and intellectuals of the landlord class began to pay attention to the study of practical problems. They wanted information on foreign countries and changes for the better in domestic politics. Gong Zizhen and Wei Yuan were their representatives.

Gong Zizhen (1792-1841) stressed the importance of reforming the feudal system. He believed that as society kept on changing, failure to conduct reforms to go with the changes was suicidal. He criticized feudal bureaucracy severely and characterized it as "lifeless and breathing its last". The feudal bureaucrats were blood suckers who drank the people's blood, he said, no different from dogs, flies, mosquitoes, and gnats, and they were as brutal as jackals and wolves. He hoped that reformers would emerge to change the lifeless, hopeless status quo.

Wei Yuan (1794-1857) also proposed the conduct of reforms. "A little reform will make the country a little better, and a big reform will make the country a lot better", he stated. He wanted China to be rich and strong and proposed ways to achieve that goal and make the country capable of resisting aggression. The most important means, said he, was "to adopt the barbarian ways to resist the barbarians". In other words, he wanted China to learn about the advanced technology of foreign countries to resist foreign aggression.

Towards the end of the 19th century, the political and social theories of the Western bourgeoisie began to arrive in China. Yan Fu (1853-1921) was the representative of those who introduced these theories to the Chinese. Among the works he translated were *The Spirit of the Laws* by Montesquieu, *Origin of Species* by Charles Darwin, *The Wealth of Nations* by Adam Smith, and some other works of the Western bourgeois scholars. All these translations had a great impact on the revolutionary movement of the Chinese bourgeoisie.

Literature and Science. In literature, many works of a patriotic content came about after the Opium War. They praised the Chinese people's heroic struggle against foreign aggression, exposed the crimes of the imperialists, and condemned the Qing rulers for their compromise and capitulation. In his poem *World*, Wei Yuan pours scorn on the Qing officials for their eagerness to surrender. In a poem entitled *Sanyuanli*, Zhang Weiping describes the patriotic sentiment and heroic deeds of the Sanyuanli masses who fought against the British invaders. The famous poet Huang Zunxian (1848-1905) wrote many patriotic, impassioned poems. In *Taiwan*, he narrates the tragedy of ceding the island to Japan and, earnestly and impassionately, asked the Taiwan people to stand side by side with the people on the mainland, so that the island, that had been opened up by our ancestors through blood and sweat, would be restored to China for good.

In addition, there were novels that revealed the seamy side of a semi-colonial and semi-feudal society towards the end of the Qing Dynasty. Historians refer to them as "novels of condemnation". The most famous among them were *Exposure of the Official World* by Li Boyuan, *Eyewitness Report on Strange Phenomena During the Past Twenty Years* by Wu Jianren, and *Flower in the Ocean of Sin* by Zeng Pu.

China lagged behind in science and technology during this period, but accomplishments were not totally absent. Wu Qijun (1789-1847) collected the ancient materials on plants and wrote *Data and Illustrations*

About Plants, in which 838 different plants were identified. Based upon his own observation, he wrote *Plants Illustrated*, in which 1,714 different plants were identified. Both were important works on botany in modern times. Zou Boqi (1819-69) summarized China's achievements in geometrical optics by writing *A Supplement to Studies on Images* in which he used mathematics to explain various theories on the formation of images through reflectors and lens, as well as basic principles relating to mirrors and glasses, including eyeglasses, telescope, and microscope. He was also versed in astronomy, astrology, geography, and surveying. His other works include *Stars on the Equator, Stars on the Ecliptic*, and *Quick Methods of Involution*.

Early in the 20th century, Zhan Tianyou (1861-1919) designed and led the construction of the Beijing-Zhangjiakou Railway. This was the first important railway designed and constructed by the Chinese. In 1908, Feng Ru (1882-1912) succeeded in making an experimental aeroplane. In June 1910, he completed the manufacturing of a plane that was well-advanced for its time. Both men worked under the most difficult circumstances, and their accomplishments testified to the great inventive ability of the Chinese people.

New Culture Movement. While in power, the Northern warlords pursued the reactionary policies of "returning to the ancient ways" and worshipping Confucius. The radical democrats, represented by Chen Duxiu (1880-1942), Li Dazhao (1889-1927), and Lu Xun (1881-1936), did their best to promote a bourgeois culture and fought fiercely against all feudal ideas. They started the New Culture Movement.

In September 1915, Chen Duxiu published *The*

Youth Magazine which was changed to *New Youth* in the autumn of 1916.   Li Dazhao and Lu Xun were among its major contributors.   This journal served as the main organ for the New Culture Movement, which advocated democracy, science, new literature, vernacular Chinese, and new ethics, while opposing feudal autocracy, superstition, old literature, classical Chinese, and old ethics.   It concentrated its attack on Confucianism, the ideological bulwark of the feudal system.   Aimed at the emancipation of the mind, the New Culture Movement encouraged the people to pursue democracy and science and seek the way whereby the nation and its people could be saved.

After China's defeat in the Opium War, progressive elements such as Hong Xiuquan, Kang Youwei, Yan Fu, and Sun Yat-sen all turned to the West in their search for truth whereby the nation could be saved.   None succeeded.   The success of Russia's October Revolution in 1917 brought to China Marxism-Leninism, and the progressive elements in China viewed this revolution as "the dawn of a new era".   They demanded that China travel the Russian road.   A number of the radical democrats gradually acquired some rudimentary communist ideas. In November 1918, Li Dazhao published in *New Youth* two articles: "The Victory of the Common People" and "The Victory of Bolshevism". In these articles he praised highly Russia's socialist revolution and then boldly pointed out: "The world of the future will be the world of the Red Flag!"

The New Culture Movement of this period still functioned within the framework of the old bourgeois democracy.   But the progressive elements of China had already begun to use Marxism as a spiritual weapon in their effort to educate and organize the revolutionary people. This paved the way for the Chinese revolution to be transformed from the old-democratic revolution into the new-democratic revolution.

Chapter Three

CONTEMPORARY PERIOD (1919-49)

During the 30 years between 1919, when the May Fourth Movement began, and 1949, when the People's Republic of China was established, China remained a semi-colonial and semi-feudal society. Led by the Chinese Communist Party, the struggle of the Chinese people against the reactionary rule in China of imperialism, feudalism, and bureaucrat-capitalism constituted the main event of this period. The event fell within the frame-work of a bourgeois democratic revolution. However, since the struggle itself was led by the proletariat and its vanguard the Chinese Communist Party, we refer to it as the new-democratic revolution as distinct from the old-democratic revolution that was led by the bourgeoisie.

1. MAY FOURTH MOVEMENT, AND ESTABLISHMENT OF THE CHINESE COMMUNIST PARTY

May Fourth Movement. After the conclusion of World War I, Britain, France, the United States, Japan, and other victors held a "peace conference" in Paris in January 1919. China, as one of the "victors", also sent a delegation. During the conference, the Chinese delegation demanded the termination of foreign countries' special privileges in China, the abolition of the Twenty-

One Demands which the Northern warlord regime had signed with Japan, and the return to China of the rights in Shandong which Japan had seized from Germany during World War I. But the peace conference turned down China's just demand. Instead, it resolved to transfer Germany's special rights in Shandong to Japan.

On May 4, 1919, more than 3,000 students in Beijing gathered on the Tiananmen Square to protest against the outrageous decision made by the Paris Peace Conference. During the demonstration that was held after the rally, they raised such slogans as "Uphold China's sovereignty! Punish the traitors!" and "No signature on the Versailles Treaty!" They demanded punishment of the pro-Japanese traitors Cao Rulin, Zhang Zongxiang, and Lu Zongyu. They burned Cao Rulin's residence and beat severely Zhang Zongxiang who was hiding in Cao's house. The next day, the students in Beijing called a strike and refused to attend classes. On the third day, all the Beijing students of and above the secondary school level formed an association. They sent out telegrams and pamphlets, organized speech-making tours to publicize their stand, and called upon all people in China to rise and join the struggle. Prompt response came from students in Tianjin, Nanjing, Shanghai, Wuhan, Changsha and Guangzhou where mammoth rallies and demonstrations were also held.

On June 3, more than 2,000 students in Beijing made speeches on current affairs in the streets, and more than 170 of them were arrested. The next day, speech-making students doubled, and the number of those arrested reached 700. The warlord government's arrest of patriotic students, a reactionary act of violence, aroused the anger of all the people in the country, and the patri-

otic movement against imperialism and warlordism spread
far and wide.

When the movement began, the principal participants were students. After June 3, the struggle developed into a patriotic movement of the proletariat, the petty
bourgeoisie, and the national bourgeoisie, with the proletariat as its main force. On June 5, the workers in
Shanghai called a general strike; by June 10, nearly
70,000 workers had joined it. Workers in many other
cities followed the example of their Shanghai colleagues
by calling strikes. Meanwhile, the merchants in Shanghai and other places closed their shops to indicate their
support.

Under the pressure of the nationwide patriotic
movement, the government of the Northern warlords re-
leased the arrested students. It dismissed from office
the three traitors and refused to sign the Versailles Peace
Treaty. Thus the struggle — the May Fourth Movement
as it came to be called — achieved its first victory.

The May Fourth Movement helped the New Culture
Movement by elevating it to a new and higher stage.
From then on, more and more progressive periodicals
were published, and the spread of Marxism became the
mainstream of the New Culture Movement. Among the
most famous periodicals were the *Xiangjiang Review* in
Changsha edited by Mao Zedong and the *Bulletin of the
Tianjin Students' Federation* edited by Zhou Enlai, apart
from the *New Youth* and *The Weekly Review* in Beijing.
In May 1919, the editors of *New Youth* published a special
issue on Marxism. Li Dazhao organized the Marxism
Study Society on Beijing University campus, Mao Zedong
and Cai Hesen established the New People Study Society
in Changsha, and Zhou Enlai founded the Awakening

Society in Tianjin. All of them were highly instrumental in the propagation of Marxism. *Manifesto of the Communist Party* and some other Marxist works were translated into Chinese during this period.

The May Fourth Movement was a resolute, uncompromising movement against imperialism and feudalism. During this movement, the Chinese proletariat ascended the political stage and demonstrated its great strength. Intellectuals who had been initiated into communist ideology provided the leadership. The May Fourth Movement helped the integration of Marxism with the Chinese working-class movement. In ideology and in organization, it paved the way for the founding of the Chinese Communist Party. It made possible the transformation of the Chinese revolution from the old-democratic to the new-democratic revolution.

Establishment of the Chinese Communist Party. The Chinese working-class movement made further progress after the May Fourth Movement. The victory of Russia's October Revolution had a profound impact on China; it provided a model for the Chinese revolution to follow. Marxism was more popularized, and gradually the time arrived for the founding of the Chinese Communist Party.

In May 1920, Chen Duxiu and others founded China's first Communist group in Shanghai. Shortly afterwards, Li Dazhao in Beijing, Mao Zedong in Hunan, Dong Biwu in Wuhan, and others in Jinan, Guangzhou, Japan, and Paris also formed their own Communist groups.

In July 1921, the Chinese Communist Party convened its First National Congress in Shanghai. Thirteen delegates attended, and they were Mao Zedong, Dong Biwu, Chen Tanqiu, He Shuheng, Wang Jinmei, Deng Enming,

Li Da, Li Hanjun, Bao Huiseng, Chen Gongbo, Zhou Fohai, Zhang Guotao, and Liu Renjing, representing about 50 Communists across the country. (The last-mentioned four delegates became renegades to the revolution at a later date.) The congress passed the Party's first constitution and elected Chen Duxiu as the Secretary-General of the Party's Central Committee. Thus the Chinese Communist Party was formally inaugurated.

In July 1922, the Chinese Communist Party convened its Second National Congress in Shanghai. The major task of this congress was to formulate the Party's programme for the Chinese revolution. The congress announced that its basic task then was "to eliminate civil strife, overthrow the warlords, and establish domestic peace; to cast off the yoke of oppression by international imperialism so that the Chinese nation can become truly independent; and to unify China into a genuine democratic republic." Thus, in the history of modern China, the Chinese Communist Party was the first to present a programme of thoroughgoing anti-imperialism and anti-feudalism for the democratic revolution. The congress also decided that the Chinese Communist Party would apply for membership of the Communist International.

First High Tide of Working-Class Movement. After its establishment, the Chinese Communist Party concentrated its effort on providing leadership to the workers' movement. It formed the Chinese Trade Union Secretariat as the headquarters that openly directed this movement. From January 1922 to February 1923, the working-class movement raged across the country, as more than 180 strikes were called, with more than 300,000 workers participating. This marked the first high tide of the worker movement in the history of China. Among the more famous strikes was that staged by 100,000 seamen in Hongkong and the strikes in the Anyuan Coal Mine of Jiangxi Province and along the Zhuzhou-Pingxiang Railway where 20,000 workers were involved.

On February 1, 1923, when the General Trade Union of the Beijing-Hankou Railway was holding its inauguration meeting at Zhengzhou, warlord Wu Peifu sabotaged the meeting. On the 4th a general strike was called, and all trains on the railway stopped moving. The strikers cried aloud: "Fight for freedom! Fight for human rights!" Instigated by the imperialists, Wu Peifu responded on the 7th by slaughtering the strikers. Thirty-seven strikers were killed, more than 200 were wounded, dozens were arrested, and more than 1,000, having been fired from their jobs, became homeless refugees. Two Communists, Lin Xiangqian and Shi Yang, were killed. This was the famous February Seventh Strike involving a massacre that shook the world. Later, as feudal warlords increased their pressure, the workers' organizations in various parts of China suffered great damages, and the working-class movement, for the time being, ebbed.

2. FIRST REVOLUTIONARY CIVIL WAR

Kuomintang-Communist Co-operation — Establishment of Revolutionary United Front. After the failure of the 1911 Revolution, the revolutionaries led by Sun Yat-sen continued their struggle for democratic revolution, but they failed each and every time. The Chinese Communist Party admired Sun's dauntless spirit and sent Li Dazhao and Lin Boqu to provide him with direct aid. Meanwhile, the Soviet Union also suggested to Sun

that a capable party uniting the workers and peasants be
established and that a military academy and a revolutionary armed force be organized too. Sun welcomed the
assistance of the Chinese Communist Party and the Soviet
Union and started to reorganize his Kuomintang. (The
China Revolutionary League was renamed Kuomintang
after the Revolution of 1911.) This step Sun took proved
to be the turning point in his life.

In June 1923, the Chinese Communist Party held its
Third National Congress in Guangzhou. The congress
resolved that the Party would co-operate with the Kuomintang and that Communists might join the Kuomintang
as individuals. The Chinese Communist Party, meanwhile, would maintain its own independence, politically,
ideologically, and organizationally.

In January 1924, Sun Yat-sen convened in Guangzhou the First National Congress of the Kuomintang. The
congress enacted a new programme and a new constitution for the party; it also agreed that Communists might
join the Kuomintang as individuals. Communists including Li Dazhao, Mao Zedong, Lin Boqu, and Qu Qiubai
participated in the congress' leadership work and were
later elected as members or alternate members of the
Kuomintang's Central Executive Committee. The congress formally adopted the three cardinal policies of
"allying with Russia, allying with the Communist Party,
and assisting the peasants and workers". Sun Yat-sen
developed his Old Three People's Principles into the New
Three People's Principles based on the three cardinal
policies. The Kuomintang's First National Congress
marked the formal beginning of the revolutionary united
front.

After the conclusion of the congress, the Kuomintang

accepted as members a large number of workers, peasants, and revolutionary intellectuals. Its composition underwent a drastic change, as it now became a revolutionary alliance of the workers, peasants, urban petty bourgeoisie, and national bourgeoisie. In May 1924, Sun Yat-sen founded in Guangzhou the Huangpu Military Academy with the assistance of the Soviet Union and the Chinese Communist Party. The Chinese Communist Party sent Zhou Enlai to serve as the director of the academy's political department, and Ye Jianying and Nie Rongzhen as instructors. Many Party and Youth League members were cadets of the academy, who later became part of the backbone force of the revolution. Then the academy's director was Chiang Kai-shek, and the resident Kuomintang representative was Liao Zhongkai.

In November 1924, Sun Yat-sen, in ill health, left Guangzhou for Beijing. He held a news conference in Shanghai during which he said: "I shall have two missions in Beijing. One is to convene a national assembly as a means to deal with the warlords. The other is to abolish the unequal treaties as a means to deal with the imperialists." On March 12, 1925, he died of illness in Beijing. In his will, he pointed out that to win freedom and equality for China among the nations, "we must bring about a thorough awakening of our own people and ally ourselves in a common struggle with those peoples of the world who treat us on the basis of equality". As a great precursor of China's democratic revolution, Sun Yat-sen devoted his life to the betterment of the country. His was a great career, and his death was mourned by all the people in China.

May 30th Movement, Guangzhou-Hongkong Strike, and Peasant Movement. After the formation of the united front, the worker and peasant movement developed quickly under the leadership of the Chinese Communist Party.

Between February and April, 1925, workers at the Japanese-run textile mills in both Shanghai and Qingdao staged strikes. On May 15, Japanese capitalists in Shanghai killed a worker named Gu Zhenghong, who was a Communist, and wounded a dozen or more other workers. On May 30, more than 10,000 students and workers in Shanghai protested and demonstrated in the city's concessions. British police opened fire at Nanjing Road; 11 of the demonstrators were killed and dozens wounded. This was the "May 30th Massacre". On June 1, more than 200,000 Shanghai workers struck in protest, 50,000 students left their classrooms, and most merchants closed their shops. Later, more than 30 cities across the country responded, giving rise to an anti-imperialist patriotic movement embracing all the people. In terms of impact, the Guangzhou-Hongkong strike was the most notable.

On June 19, 1925, a strike involving more than 100,000 workers exploded in Hongkong, and the strikers then left for Guangzhou one after another. On June 23, the returned strikers joined the workers, peasants, students, and cadets of the Huangpu Military Academy — totalling more than 100,000 — to stage a massive demonstration in Guangzhou. British sailors and police opened fire, killing 52 persons on the spot, and wounding a large number of others. On June 29, the strikers in Hongkong increased to 250,000. About 130,000 of them returned to Guangzhou where they intended to conduct a protracted struggle. The Guangzhou-Hongkong Strike Committee, organized by workers in both cities, formed an armed picket corps of more than 2,000 men that cut off supplies to Hongkong and made it a "dead port". The strike lasted until October 10, 1926, for a period of 16 months. As one of the longest strikes in the world, it dealt a severe blow to the imperialist influence in south China, and it helped enormously in consolidating the province of Guangdong as a revolutionary base and in preparing for the launching of the Northern Expedition.

During this period, the peasant movement, under the leadership of the Chinese Communist Party, also made rapid progress. The rapidest progress was made by the peasant movement in Guangdong under the leadership of Peng Pai, a Communist. In January 1926, the peasant association in Guangdong had a membership of 620,000, and the peasant self-defence corps 30,000. In February 1925, Mao Zedong returned to his native place Shaoshan, Hunan Province, where he led a peasant movement and succeeded in organizing peasant associations in more than 20 townships. In June 1926, 12 of China's provinces had peasant associations, numbering 5,300 of and above the township level. Total membership was about one million.

Consolidation of Guangdong Revolutionary Base and Usurpation of Power by Chiang Kai-shek. After its establishment, the revolutionary regime in Guangdong soon wiped out all the warlords and unified the province. On July 1, 1925, the National Government formally came into existence in Guangzhou. On August 26, all the army units belonging to the National Government were reorganized as the National Revolutionary Army. The student soldiers of the Huangpu Military Academy became its First Army, with Zhou Enlai as director of its political department. Each army unit had a Party representative and a political department. Many Communists were appointed Party representatives responsible for political work in the various units.

After the death of Sun Yat-sen, the split within the Kuomintang gradually became more evident. A section of the Kuomintang members continued to adhere to Sun's three cardinal policies of "allying with Russia, allying with the Communist Party, and assisting the peasants and workers", and they were known as the Left wing of the Kuomintang. Another section, who represented the interest of the big landlords and comprador bourgeoisie, opposed these policies, and they were referred to as the Right wing of the Kuomintang. The struggle between the two wings was very intense. Towards the end of 1925, a section of the Right wing openly left the Kuomintang and formed a counter-revolutionary faction known as the "Western Hills Conference Group". It acquired this name in November 1925 when its members held a conference next to Sun Yat-sen's mausoleum in the Western Hills of Beijing, where they made public their counter-revolutionary stand. With Chiang Kai-shek as their representative, the Kuomintang Rightists, disguising themselves as revolutionaries, used all kinds of devious methods and schemes and thus gradually usurped the power of the Kuomintang and of the army. At the beginning of the Northern Expedition, he was chairman of the Standing Committee of the Kuomintang's Central Executive Committee and concurrently head of its Department of Organization and Department of Soldiers' Affairs, as well as chairman of the Military Affairs Commission of the National Government and commander-in-chief of the National Revolutionary Army.

Northern Expedition and High Tide of Worker and Peasant Movement. On July 1, 1926, the National Government issued a "Declaration on the Northern Expedition" and so launched the punitive expedition against the Northern warlords. Its main targets were Wu Peifu who occupied Hunan, Hubei, and Henan; Sun Chuanfang who controlled Jiangsu, Anhui, Zhejiang, Fujian, and Jiangxi; and Zhang Zuolin, the overlord of the northeastern provinces plus Beijing and Tianjin.

In May 1926, the Independent Regiment, commanded by Ye Ting and staffed mostly by the Communists and Youth League members, marched to the front in Hunan as the vanguard unit of the Northern Expedition. On July 9, eight armies of approximately 100,000 men left Guangzhou on three separate routes.

The main battlefields of the Northern Expedition were Hunan and Hubei. The Northern Expeditionary Army quickly took Changsha and Yuezhou and, at the strategic points along the Guangzhou-Hankou Railway, Dingsiqiao and Heshengqiao, destroyed Wu Peifu's main force. In September and October, it captured the triple city of Wuhan and won decisively the battle of Hunan and Hubei. Meanwhile, the troops moving along the other two routes occupied Nanchang, Jiujiang, Anqing, and Nanjing. Thus, in less than six months, the Northern Expeditionary Army had overthrown the two biggest warlords, Wu Peifu and Sun Chuanfang. The revolution had moved from Guangdong to the Changjiang River valley, covering half of China. In the middle of December, the National Government and the Central Executive Committee of the Kuomintang moved from Guangzhou to Wuhan.

The victory of the Northern Expedition sped up the development of the peasant movement. The struggle in Hunan, organized and led by Mao Zedong, became the

core of the peasant movement in the whole country. All
across China, in Hubei, Jiangxi, Guangdong, Fujian,
Zhejiang, Henan, and other provinces, the movement
developed with great momentum. In March 1927, membership of the peasant associations exceeded 10 million.

The revolutionary struggle waged by the workers
also developed rapidly. In January 1927, workers in
Wuhan, led by Liu Shaoqi, succeeded in restoring to China the British Concession in that city. Later, workers
in Jiujiang of Jiangxi Province did likewise. To co-
ordinate their activities with the Northern Expeditionary
Army in its victorious march, the workers in Shanghai
staged armed uprisings thrice. The first two uprisings,
in October 1926 and February 1927, failed. However,
the third uprising that began on March 21, 1927 under the
leadership of Zhou Enlai and others, succeeded after more
than 30 hours of bloody battle. Finally, Shanghai was
liberated.

**Kuomintang Rightists' Betrayal, and Failure of the
First Revolutionary Civil War.** The victory of the
Northern Expedition and the rapid development of the
worker and peasant movement shook the imperialist rule
in China. On March 24, 1927, after the Northern Expeditionary Army had occupied Nanjing, the warships of
Britain, the United States, France, Japan, and Italy, then
anchored nearby, bombarded the city with artillery fire
and killed and wounded more than 2,000 persons. This
massacre indicated clearly the imperialists' scheme to in-
terfere with the Chinese revolution by military means
and to compel the Chinese bourgeoisie to betray the revolution. They selected Chiang Kai-shek as their new
agent and attempted to destroy the revolution from within. Chiang, on his part, responded by collaborating

more closely with the imperialists, the landlords, and the compradors. On April 12, 1927, he staged a counter-revolutionary coup in Shanghai and carried out a mass slaughter of workers and Communists. The same happened in Jiangsu, Zhejiang, Fujian, Guangdong, and other provinces. On April 18, Chiang Kai-shek established in Nanjing his so-called "National Government" that represented no one except the big landlord class and the big bourgeoisie.

The betrayal by Chiang Kai-shek caused only partial failure of the revolution. The National Government in Wuhan still had enough strength to control three provinces: Hubei, Hunan, and Jiangxi. However, at this crucial moment, the leader of the Chinese Communist Party, Chen Duxiu, stubbornly carried out a line of Right opportunism and thought only alliance to the denial of struggle in his interpretation of the Party's united front policy. He made one concession after another to the increasingly reactionary Wang Jingwei faction of the Kuomintang in Wuhan and even condoned the suppression of the worker-peasant movement by the reactionary forces and ordered the disarmament of the workers' picket corps and the peasants' self-defence corps. His erroneous line enhanced the arrogance of the counter-revolutionaries. On July 15, Wang Jingwei convened in Wuhan a conference at which he formally announced his break with the Chinese Communist Party and betrayed the revolution. He went so far as to put forward the reactionary slogan, "Better kill one thousand non-Communists by mistake than allow a single true Communist to slip through the net." Then he killed Communists and other revolutionaries on a massive scale. This was the counter-revolutionary coup of July 15, 1927, after which Chiang Kai-shek and Wang Jingwei joined hands. Thus the First Revolutionary Civil War ended in failure.

Nevertheless, the Chinese Communist Party wrote a brilliant chapter during this revolutionary civil war by leading all the Chinese people in the great struggle against imperialism and feudalism. Due to the enormous combined strength of the imperialists, the feudal warlords, and the reactionary clique of the Kuomintang and especially due to the predominance of Chen Duxiu's Right opportunist line in the leading organ of the Chinese Communist Party at the later stage, the revolution failed. The First Revolutionary Civil War taught a valuable lesson: that the democratic revolution in China must be led by the working class and carried out through a revolutionary united front also led by the working class; that the central issue concerning working-class leadership was the peasant question, and that the working class could win victory in the revolution only when it had the peasantry as its revolutionary ally; and that the principal form of the Chinese revolution could only be that of an armed revolution vis-à-vis an armed counter-revolution, and that without a revolutionary army there would be no revolution.

3. SECOND REVOLUTIONARY CIVIL WAR

Establishment of the People's Army. Nanchang Uprising, Autumn Harvest Uprising, and Guangzhou Uprising. After the failure of the First Revolutionary Civil War, the Kuomintang of Chiang Kai-shek replaced the Northern warlords by establishing a nationwide reactionary regime that represented the interest of the big landlord class and the big bourgeoisie. The revolutionaries, however, were not cowed, or overcome, or totally wiped out, despite the White terror. To save the revolution, the Chinese Communist Party decided to stage armed uprisings.

On August 1, 1927, 30,000 men of the Northern Expeditionary Army, who either were led or had been influenced by the Chinese Communist Party, staged an armed uprising in Nanchang, Jiangxi Province. The uprising was led by Zhou Enlai (then Secretary of Party's Front Committee), Zhu De, He Long, Ye Ting, Liu Bocheng, and others. After five hours of fierce battle, the insurgents succeeded in killing all the more than 10,000 Kuomintang garrison troops. Several days later, they moved southward across Jiangxi and made plans to seize Guangzhou and re-establish the revolutionary base of Guangdong Province. Early in October, they were surrounded in eastern Guangdong by a superior force of the enemy's and suffered heavy casualties. One contingent, led by Zhu De and Chen Yi, moved to Hunan to continue the struggle. The Nanchang Uprising marked the beginning of armed struggle independently led by the Chinese Communist Party — the first shot that the revolutionary army fired at the Kuomintang reactionaries. The day of August 1, from then on, has been celebrated as the birthday of the Chinese people's revolutionary army.

On August 7, 1927, the Central Committee of the Chinese Communist Party held an emergency meeting in Hankou, presided over by Qu Qiubai. The meeting criticized and corrected Chen Duxiu's Right opportunism and relieved him of his leadership role in the Central Committee. A new provisional Political Bureau was elected. The meeting adopted the policy of agrarian revolution and of armed opposition to the reactionary rule of the Kuomintang. It also drafted a plan for autumn harvest uprisings in Hunan, Hubei, Jiangxi and Guangdong provinces.

After the August Seventh Conference, the Central Committee sent Mao Zedong to the Jiangxi-Hunan border to lead an autumn harvest uprising. The uprising exploded on September 9. The revolutionary army of workers and peasants moved along three routes in a converging attack on Changsha. It suffered heavy losses, however, due to the greater strength of the enemy. Analysing the situation, Mao Zedong believed that the revolutionary army should no longer attack key cities where the enemy was strong but should instead concentrate its effort on the countryside where the enemy was weak. He, therefore, led the remaining forces to the Jinggang Mountains located between the provinces of Hunan and Jiangxi.

On December 11, 1927, an uprising was staged in Guangzhou under the leadership of Zhang Tailei, Ye Ting, and Ye Jianying and with the Training Corps of the Fourth Army of the Northern Expeditionary Army and the Workers' Red Guards of Guangzhou as backbone. They established a democratic government of the workers and peasants. However, it soon proved impossible to attempt to seize large cities when the enemy was so much stronger. Surrounded and attacked by the imperialists and the Kuomintang warlords, the Guangzhou Uprising quickly collapsed. The insurgent troops that were withdrawn from Guangzhou later joined the armed forces of peasant rebels in Guangdong and Guangxi to continue the struggle.

The Nanchang, Autumn Harvest, and Guangzhou uprisings dealt a resounding blow at the policy of mass slaughter pursued by the Kuomintang. The Chinese Communist Party then entered a new period during which the Workers' and Peasants' Red Army was created.

Establishment and Development of Rural Revolutionary Bases. In October 1927, the revolutionary army of the workers and peasants, led by Mao Zedong, arrived at the Jinggang Mountains area. In this area, they mobilized the masses to carry on a guerrilla warfare, initiated an agrarian revolution, and established local armed forces, Party organizations, and a workers' and peasants' regime. The Jinggang Mountains proved to be the first revolutionary base in the rural areas of China. In April 1928, an army contingent that had participated in the Nanchang Uprising and the contingent of armed peasants that had taken part in the uprisings in Hunan, led by Zhu De and Chen Yi, arrived at the Jinggang Mountains and joined forces with the revolutionary army led by Mao Zedong. After their meeting, these forces were reorganized into the Fourth Army of the Chinese Workers' and Peasants' Red Army, numbering more than 10,000 men. Zhu De served as its commander, Mao Zedong as the Party representative, and Chen Yi as the director of its political department. During the war in defence of the Jinggang Mountains area, Zhu De and Mao Zedong created the famous guerrilla tactics that was summarized as follows: "The enemy advances, we retreat; the enemy camps, we harass; the enemy tires, we attack; the enemy retreats, we pursue". It was during the period of struggle in the Jinggang Mountains that the principle of the Party's absolute leadership over the army was established. The Red Army was required to fulfil three tasks: fighting, raising money for the revolutionary cause (later changed to production), and mass work. The "Three Main Rules of Discipline" and the "Eight Points for Attention"[1] were also formulated for the people's army at this time.

From the autumn of 1927 to 1930, the Red Army and revolutionary bases across China underwent a process of gradual expansion. In January 1929, Mao Zedong and Zhu De led the Red Army's Fourth Army to southern Jiangxi where they established two revolutionary bases, Southern Jiangxi and Western Fujian. In 1930, the Central Revolutionary Base was established in Ruijin, Jiangxi Province. By the first half of 1930, the Chinese Communist Party had staged armed uprisings in more than 300 counties and established 15 revolutionary bases. By then, the Red Army across the country had grown to 60,000 men.

As the rural revolutionary bases were established and grew, the agrarian revolution was carried out with great enthusiasm. This meant the overthrow of the

---

[1] These rules and points later went through some changes until they were finalized in 1947 as follows:

1. The Three Main Rules of Discipline:
    (1) Obey orders in all your actions.
    (2) Don't take a single needle or piece of thread from the masses.
    (3) Turn in everything captured.
2. The Eight Points for Attention:
    (1) Speak politely.
    (2) Pay fairly for what you buy.
    (3) Return everything you borrow.
    (4) Pay for anything you damage.
    (5) Don't hit or swear at people.
    (6) Don't damage crops.
    (7) Don't take liberties with women.
    (8) Don't ill-treat captives.

landlords and the distribution of land among the peasants.
As a result, the Chinese Communist Party won heartfelt
support from the peasants many of whom joined the Red
Army of their own accord.   The Red Army and the revolutionary bases became invulnerable.

The establishment and development of the Jinggang
Mountains and other rural revolutionary bases opened up
a new road to the Chinese revolution, namely, the road of
establishing and developing such bases and then encircling and finally seizing the cities from the countryside
for the nationwide victory of the revolution.   In the two
articles, "Why Is It That Red Political Power Can Exist
in China?" and "A Single Spark Can Start a Prairie Fire",
written in 1928 and 1930 respectively, Mao Zedong explained the reason why the red regime could survive in
China.   He pointed out that China, a semi-colonial country indirectly controlled by the imperialists, was extremely unbalanced in its political and economic development.   ". . . A localized agricultural economy (not a
unified capitalist economy) and the imperialist policy of
marking off spheres of influence in order to divide and
exploit" and the resultant "prolonged splits and wars
within the White regime"[1] combined to weaken the reactionary rule in remote countryside and enable the Red
areas to emerge, persist and develop amidst the encirclement of the White regime.   He further pointed out that
the establishment of revolutionary bases and political
power in rural areas, the thorough implementation of the
agrarian revolution, and the development of armed
struggle — all this was prerequisite to the strategy of

---

[1] "Why Is It That Red Political Power Can Exist in China?"
Selected Works of Mao Zedong, Foreign Languages Press, Beijing,
1975, Vol. I, p. 65.

marching to the countryside, building the revolutionary forces there and encircling the cities from the villages for the final nationwide victory of the revolutionary cause. The history of the Chinese revolution proved correct Mao Zedong's theory, a theory that was in conformity with the reality of China.

The development of the Red Army and the rural revolutionary bases aroused the fear and hatred the Kuomintang government. Chiang Kai-shek mobilized large troops to conduct his "encirclement and suppression" campaigns against them. From December 1930 to September 1931, he carried out three such campaigns on a large scale against the Central Revolutionary Base. Under the correct leadership of the local Party organization and Mao Zedong, the Red Army defeated each and every one of them. The Red Army became larger and stronger; so did the revolutionary bases.

Struggle Against Japanese Imperialist Aggression. While Chiang Kai-shek was devoting all his energy to prosecuting the civil war, the Japanese imperialists, on September 18, 1931, used troops to occupy Shenyang, thus precipitating the September Eighteenth Incident. Chiang's order that under no circumstances should the Northeastern Army resist enabled the enemy to take over the three northeastern provinces, covering an area of more than one million square kilometres, in a little more than three months.

On January 18, 1932, the Japanese aggressors launched a surprise attack on Shanghai. Under the leadership of Cai Tingkai and Jiang Guangnai, the Nineteenth Route Army, then stationed there, rose and fought and dealt a severe blow to the aggressors. However, due to the betrayal by the Kuomintang authorities, the heroic resistance lasted only a little more than one month before it collapsed.

As the Japanese imperialists intensified their aggression, the crisis China faced became graver and graver. In September 1931 and again in January 1933, the Chinese Communist Party issued statements calling for "the mobilization of the masses to resist Japanese imperialist aggression". In no time, the anti-Japanese democratic movement, led by the Chinese Communist Party, spread across the country. In the northeastern provinces, armed anti-Japanese forces were formed one after another. From 1934 onward, these forces were gradually unified as the Allied Anti-Japanese Army of the Northeast, led by the Chinese Communist Party and commanded by Yang Jingyu, Zhou Baozhong and Li Zhaolin. Early in 1937, the Allied Army had as many as 45,000 men, controlling more than one-half of the northeastern provinces. It tied up much of the Japanese forces that otherwise would have been committed against China proper. It struck blow after blow to Japan's colonial rule in the northeastern provinces.

Long March and Zunyi Conference. After the Kuomintang's three "encirclement and suppression" campaigns were crushed, the revolutionary bases across China expanded to embrace more than 300 counties, with a total population of several tens of millions. People's governments were established at the primary level on these bases. On November 7, 1931, the Chinese Communist Party convened in Ruijin, Jiangxi Province, the First National Congress of Workers, Peasants and Soldiers and formed a Central Democratic Government of Workers and Peasants with Mao Zedong as Chairman and Zhu De commander-in-chief of its armed forces. Ruijin was chosen as the capital of Red China.

In February 1933, at a time when Japan was launching an all-out aggression against China, Chiang Kai-shek, disregarding the survival of the nation, mobilized 500,000 men to commence his fourth "encirclement and suppression" campaign against the Central Revolutionary Base. Once again, he was defeated. By 1933, the Red Army had grown to 300,000 men.

In January 1931, Wang Ming (originally known as Chen Shaoyu, 1904-74) seized leadership in the Party at the Fourth Plenary Session of its Sixth Central Committee. From that time to 1934, he promoted within the Party a "Left" opportunist line characterized by doctrinairism, which did great damage to the revolution. He stubbornly insisted on the seizing of big cities and opposed the strategy of encircling the cities from the countryside and seizing power by armed forces. He and his like wanted the Red Army to occupy the major cities immediately and ordered the staging of strikes and demonstrations by workers and students in the large cities controlled by the Kuomintang. As a result, nearly all the Party organizations in the Kuomintang areas were destroyed. Wang Ming and his followers adopted a policy of "ruthless struggle" and "merciless blows" towards those comrades who disagreed with them. Mao Zedong himself was at one time squeezed out from the leadership position in the Red Army.

In October 1933, Chiang Kai-shek mobilized one million men to conduct the fifth "encirclement and suppression" campaign against the Central Revolutionary Base and the neighbouring Hunan-Jiangxi and Fujian-Zhejiang-Jiangxi bases. Because of the "Left" opportunists' opposition to what they called "guerrillaism", the flexible tactics of concentrating a superior force, luring the enemy deep into our territory and conducting a mobile warfare were abandoned. As the Red Army was forced to fight pitched battles against a much superior enemy, it found itself in a passive position and, despite one year of struggle, failed to thwart the enemy's "encirclement and suppression" campaign and had to leave the Central Revolutionary Base for a strategic shift. In October 1934, the Red Army's First Front Army (also known as the Central Red Army) of 80,000 men left Changting and Ninghua of Fujian and Ruijin and Yudu of Jiangxi to begin the Long March. Breaking through four rings of blockade, the Red Army went through Guangdong, Hunan, and Guangxi to enter Guizhou. During the Long March, because the "Left" opportunists advocated retreat in front of strong foe, time and again the Red Army found itself in danger and it suffered heavy casualties until only less than 50 per cent of its men remained.

To rescue the Red Army and the revolution from the danger they were in, the Party's Central Committee convened in Zunyi, Guizhou Province, an enlarged meeting of its Political Bureau in January 1935. During the meeting, Wang Ming's military line of "Left" opportunism was criticized, and the correct military line with Mao Zedong as its exponent was re-established. The leadership structure of the Party was reorganized, and Mao Zedong, Zhou Enlai, and Wang Jiaxiang were elected as members of the leading group in charge of military affairs. The meeting established Mao Zedong's leadership position in the Party.   From then on, the Chinese revolution was on a victorious path.

After the Zunyi Conference, the Red Army entered northwestern Sichuan where it joined forces with the Fourth Front Army commanded by Zhang Guotao. Led by Mao Zedong, the Party and the Red Army opposed Zhang Guotao's criminal activities of splitting them, and the army was ordered to continue its northward march. After much hardship and fierce struggle, the Red Army arrived at the base area in northern Shaanxi in October 1935.   There it joined forces with the Red troops already there.   The unprecedented Long March, 12,500 kilometres in distance, was finally completed.   In October 1936, the Second Front Army and part of the Fourth Front Army, led by He Long, Ren Bishi, and others, also arrived in northern Shaanxi to join forces with the Central Red Army.

December Ninth Movement and Xi'an Incident.   In 1935, Japan moved huge troops south of the Great Wall, threatening Beiping (Beijing) and Tianjin. Its purpose was to transform north China into a Japanese colony. In June, the Kuomintang sent He Yingqin, head of the pro-Japanese clique, to sign a secret agreement with Umezu, then commander-in-chief of Japan's armed forces in north China. Under the He-Umezu Agreement, China agreed to withdraw its troops from Hebei and ban all anti-Japanese activities.   Then Japan bought Chinese traitors and proceeded with the plot of the "autonomy of the five north China provinces".   The situation in north China had become critical.

On December 9, 1935, the students in Beiping, under the leadership of the Chinese Communist Party, demonstrated in opposition to Chiang Kai-shek's policy of selling out north China. They cried aloud: "Down with Japanese imperialism!", "Oppose the autonomy of north China!" and "Stop the civil war and unite against alien aggression!" But they encountered suppression from the Kuomintang troops and police. On December 16, more than 30,000 students and other citizens in Beiping gathered and demonstrated, and their struggle received sympathy and support across the nation. Many students took off their uniforms and went to the factories and villages to organize the masses and propagandize for the anti-Japanese cause. The December Ninth Movement marked a new high tide in the effort against Japanese aggression and for national salvation.

After the north China incident, the contradiction between the Chinese nation and Japanese imperialism became the principal contradiction, overshadowing for the time being the class contradiction at home. In December 1935, the Chinese Communist Party held a Political Bureau meeting in Wayaobao, north Shaanxi. It criticized the "Leftist" mistake of refusing to unite with all forces that could be united with, and adopted the policy of a national united front against Japanese aggression.

As the resist-Japan-and-save-the-nation movement built to a climax, patriotic soldiers among the Kuomintang ranks were deeply influenced. The Northeastern Army led by Zhang Xueliang and the Northwestern Army led by Yang Hucheng, both of which had been sent by Chiang Kai-shek to northern Shaanxi to attack the Red Army, had actually effected a cease fire with it. Angered and frightened by the changed attitude of Zhang and Yang, Chiang personally went to Xi'an to force them to renew the attack. On December 12, 1936, Zhang and Yang sent troops to arrest him. The next day, they sent telegrams across the country, demanding cessation of the civil war and the formation of an alliance with the Communist Party to resist Japan. This was the Xi'an Incident. However, He Yingqin's pro-Japanese clique within the Kuomintang tried to use this opportunity to enlarge the civil war, so as to facilitate Japan's aggression against China. Besides, He Yingqin wanted to wrest power from Chiang Kai-shek. He, therefore, sent troops to attack Tongguan east of Xi'an. The Chinese Communist Party, acting on behalf of the national interest and the cause of unity against Japanese aggression, resolutely opposed He Yingqin's evil scheme and proposed instead a peaceful solution of the Xi'an Incident. It sent a delegation, headed by Zhou Enlai, to Xi'an to mediate. Chiang Kai-shek was forced to accept a number of conditions, including the cessation of the civil war and the formation of an alliance with the Communist Party for resistance against Japan, before he was freed from captivity. The peaceful solution of the Xi'an Incident marked the end of 10 years of civil war and the beginning of an anti-Japanese national united front.

4. WAR OF RESISTANCE AGAINST JAPAN

Beginning of the Anti-Japanese War and Formation of the Anti-Japanese National United Front. On July 7, 1937, the aggressive forces of Japan attacked Lugouqiao (Marco Polo Bridge), located to the southwest of Beiping, and Chinese defenders responded by fighting back. This has been known as the Lugouqiao Incident, which marked the beginning of Japan's all-out aggression against China and of China's War of Resistance Against Japan.

The day after the Lugouqiao Incident, the Chinese Communist Party issued a proclamation calling upon all Chinese to join the war of resistance. To speed up the formal establishment of an anti-Japanese national united front, the Party, on July 15, issued a declaration calling for co-operation between the Communist Party and the Kuomintang, and sent Zhou Enlai to Lushan, Jiangxi Province, to talk with Chiang Kai-shek.

On August 13, Japanese troops attacked Shanghai and threatened Nanjing, posing a direct menace to Chiang Kai-shek's rule and also to the British and American interest in China. Only then was the Kuomintang government forced to participate in the war against Japan and come to an agreement with the Chinese Communist Party on joint resistance. In observation of the agreement, the main force of the Red Army, then located in the northwest and numbering about 30,000 men, was renamed the Eighth Route Army of the National Revolutionary Army, with Zhu De as commander-in-chief, Peng Dehuai as deputy commander-in-chief, and Ye Jianying as chief-of-staff. It commanded three divisions: the 115th, the 120th, and the 129th. Later, the Red guerrilla forces in the southern provinces were reorganized as the New Fourth Army, of which Ye Ting was the commander. In September, the Kuomintang made public a declaration for Kuomintang-Communist co-operation and recognized the legal status of the Chinese Communist Party. Thus the Anti-Japanese National United Front formally came into existence.

Collapse of the Kuomintang Front and Establishment of the Anti-Japanese Bases in Enemy's Rear. Resisting Japanese aggression was not a decision made willingly by the Kuomintang government, which was afraid of mobilizing the Chinese people for this effort. It was even more afraid that the Chinese Communist Party might arouse the masses for the anti-Japanese cause. It merely wanted to use the forces of Japan to reduce the strength of the resisters. With this kind of thinking to guide its action, it was defeated time and again on the battlefield by the Japanese invaders. In less than one month, it lost first Beiping and then Tianjin. By March 1938, almost all of north China fell into the enemy's hands. In November 1937, Japan occupied Shanghai. In December, it captured Nanjing. In October 1938, Guangzhou and Wuhan also fell. The Kuomintang government was forced to move its capital to Chongqing, Sichuan Province. It also moved its major forces to China's southwest and northwest so as to conserve their strength, avoiding fighting as much as it could. Wherever the Japanese invaders went, they burned, killed, and pillaged, and there was no evil they would not do. Countless cities and towns were reduced to ashes, and millions of people were butchered. Take Nanjing as an example. In a little more than one month, the invaders killed 300,000 people and burned one-third of the city's houses.

Contrary to the Kuomintang, the Chinese Communist Party mobilized the people of all strata to participate in the war of resistance. The Eighth Route Army, numbering more than 30,000 men, crossed the Huanghe River from Shaanxi and moved eastward until it reached the front of north China. In the later part of September, its 115th Division killed 3,000 of the enemy's troops at Pingxingguan, Shanxi Province. This was the first great victory after the war of resistance began, and the victory heartened the people across the nation. Later, the units of the Eighth Route Army marched to the enemy-occupied territories where they carried out guerrilla warfare, and established anti-Japanese bases. Thus the enemy's rear became the front of the anti-Japanese war. Anti-Japanese bases were established in the border regions of Shanxi, Qahar and Hebei, of Shanxi, Hebei, Shandong and Henan, of Shanxi and Suiyuan, and also in the central section of Shandong. In south China, the New Fourth Army moved north and south of the Changjiang River and established anti-Japanese bases in southern Jiangsu and also north of the river. Further to the south, the Dongjiang and Qiongya Anti-Japanese Bases were established in Guangdong. In 1938, the Eighth Route Army and the New Fourth Army tied up 400,000 Japanese troops, more than one-half of the enemy's total strength in China. These two armies were in fact the main force in the war of resistance against Japan.

In each of the anti-Japanese bases, the Chinese Communist Party established a democratic government, armed the masses, and carried out a programme of rent and interest reduction. As a result, the bases behind the enemy lines became the principal battlefields during the war of resistance and were the principal areas from which to launch strategic counter-offensive. In the revolutionary base of northern Shaanxi was established the Government of the Shaanxi-Gansu-Ningxia Border Region, which became the general rear area of all the anti-Japanese bases. Yan'an, where the headquarters of the Chinese Communist Party was located, was the centre of command for the nationwide anti-Japanese war. As the centre of the Chinese revolution, it drew millions of patriotic youths.

Communist Party's Strategy of Protracted War.

Facing a savage aggressor like Japan, the pro-Japanese clique headed by Wang Jingwei kept on harping the theme that China could be exterminated as a nation if it insisted on resisting Japan which was so much superior in military strength. On the other hand, the Chiang Kai-shek clique dreamed of relying on the strength of Britain and the United States for a quick victory. To refute both fallacies, and to point out the correct path to follow, Mao Zedong, in May 1938, wrote and made public a treatise entitled *On Protracted War,* in which he analysed the basic characteristics of both sides of the Sino-Japanese war. He pointed out that China could not win a quick victory, but that it would surely be victorious after a long period of struggle. He stressed that China's resistance war was a protracted one which would pass through the three stages of strategic defence, strategic stalemate, and strategic counter-offensive before the materialization of final victory. Particularly, he emphasized the paramount importance of a people's war. He said that "the army and the people are the foundation of victory" and that "the richest source of power to wage war lies in the masses of the people".[1] The history of the Sino-Japanese war proved correct his prediction.

Defeat of Kuomintang's Three Anti-Communist Onslaughts. The development of the guerrilla war and the anti-Japanese bases led by the Chinese Communist Party seriously threatened the security of enemy-occupied territories. After capturing Wuhan and Guangzhou in October 1938, Japan in fact had little strength to advance further, and the war entered the stage of strategic stalemate. Then Japan changed its tactics. On the

---

[1] *Selected Works of Mao Zedong,* FLP, Beijing, 1975, Vol. II, pp. 183, 186.

one hand, it concentrated its effort on attacking the Communist-led anti-Japanese bases; on the other hand, it offered the Kuomintang political inducements backed by the threat or actual use of military force. On December 22, 1938, the Japanese prime minister Konoye made the Kuomintang government a tempting offer to surrender, based on the so-called three principles. The three principles were "good-neighbour relations", "joint effort against the Communists", and "economic co-operation". Wang Jingwei left Chongqing, declared his support of Konoye's offer, and openly switched to the Japanese side. In March 1940, he set up in Nanjing a puppet regime under the direction of Japanese imperialism. The Chiang Kai-shek clique within the Kuomintang, which served the interests of Britain and the United States, wavered even more. It adopted a policy of actively opposing communism and passively opposing Japanese imperialism. It secretly negotiated with Japan on the terms of surrender, while concentrating all its effort on fighting against communism.

From the winter of 1939 to the summer of 1943, Chiang Kai-shek launched three anti-Communist onslaughts. The Chinese Communist Party, for the purpose of self-defence, smashed the Kuomintang's attack in each case. Its attitude towards the united front was that of unity and struggle and the employment of struggle to attain the goal of unity. While proceeding with struggle, it followed the tactical principles of "justifiability", "benefit" and "restraint", and the principle of resolute self-defence: "We will not attack unless we are attacked; if we are attacked, we will certainly counter-attack." Consequently, the Party defeated all the Kuomintang onslaughts.

Defence of the Liberated Areas, 1941-42. In 1941-
42, the Japanese imperialists mobilized 64 per cent of
their armed forces in China, plus nearly all the forces of
their Chinese collaborators, to launch savage "mopping-
up operations" against the anti-Japanese bases. Their
policy was known as "Three Alls": kill all, burn all, and
loot all. Slowly and gradually, they wanted to wipe out
all the bases of the guerrillas. Meanwhile, the Kuomintang forces intensified their blockade of the Liberated
Areas. Chiang Kai-shek even ordered part of his troops
to surrender purposely to Japan, so these troops, too,
could be used by Japan to attack the Liberated Areas.
The attack by the combined forces of the Japanese invaders, the puppet army, and the Kuomintang troops —
plus three years of drought in north China — brought to
the Liberated Areas the greatest difficulties between 1941
and 1942.

To overcome these difficulties, the people and
soldiers in the Liberated Areas devoted themselves to
the increase of production. All the cadres and soldiers
participated in the opening up of wilderness for crop
cultivation, the raising of hogs, and the making of cloth.
Even leaders of the Central Committee of the Chinese
Communist Party, such as Mao Zedong, Zhou Enlai, and
Zhu De, did likewise. After much hard work, many
army units and offices succeeded in attaining total or
partial self-sufficiency, improvement of livelihood, and
reduction of burden upon the people. Meanwhile, the
Party launched a rectification campaign by promoting
among all its members and cadres an education in Marxism-Leninism. In the course of this campaign, Wang
Ming's erroneous line, which had brought enormous damage to the Party, was repudiated and the ideological

level of the Party members and cadres was considerably raised. At the same time, people's militias and armed work corps were organized extensively, and every available means was employed to strike against the enemy. By effort like this, the most difficult problems in the Liberated Areas were resolved by 1943, after which these areas continued to advance. In the Kuomintang-controlled areas, on the other hand, there was political corruption of the worst type. People's livelihood deteriorated fast, complaints multiplied, and revolts were commonplace.

The Party's Seventh Congress and Victory over Japan. In the wake of the Allies' victorious campaign against the fascists across the globe, the Liberated Areas in China also launched, in 1944, partial counter-offensives and won important victories against Japan. By the spring of 1945, the nation had 19 Liberated Areas with a total population of 95 million. The regular army in these areas had grown to 910,000 men, supported by people's militias numbering 2.2 million. The Japanese invaders had retreated to the large cities along the railways, completely surrounded by the Liberated Areas.

To win final victory over Japan and to prepare for the final victory of the Chinese revolution, the Chinese Communist Party convened in Yan'an the historically significant Seventh National Congress between April 23 and June 11, 1945. Attending the congress were 752 delegates and alternates who represented 1.21 million Party members across the nation. The congress adopted an integral programme and a correct line: "Boldly mobilize the masses, defeat the Japanese aggressors, and build a new China." It also adopted a new Party constitution and elected a new Central Committee headed by Mao

Zedong. After the congress, the people's army continued
to intensify the counter-offensive until it recovered large
territories. On August 8, 1945, the Soviet Union declared war on Japan, and its Red Army attacked the
Japanese aggressors in China's northeastern provinces.
Meanwhile, the people's army in the Liberated Areas
counter-attacked on a grand scale. On August 14, Japan
surrendered unconditionally. On September 2, it signed
the instrument of surrender. The Chinese people, after
eight years of bitter struggle, finally won victory in the
anti-Japanese war.

5. THIRD REVOLUTIONARY CIVIL WAR

**Chongqing Talks and War of Self-Defence in Lib-
erated Areas.** After victory over Japan, all the people
in China demanded the creation of an independent, peaceful, democratic, prosperous, and strong China. But the
Kuomintang, headed by Chiang Kai-shek, wanted to continue its autocratic rule over the Chinese people so that
China would remain a semi-colonial and semi-feudal
country under the dictatorship of the big landlord class
and the big bourgeoisie. The United States, on its part,
wished to transform China into an American colony. The
Kuomintang of Chiang Kai-shek, colluding with U.S.
imperialism, made preparations to launch an anti-Communist and anti-people war on a large scale.

Facing a strong enemy of this kind, the Chinese Communist Party adopted a policy of "giving him tit for tat
and fighting for every inch of land". On the one hand,
it did its best to win peace and oppose war; on the other,

it made full preparations for beating back every military attack by the Kuomintang.

Because of the enormous strength of the army and people in the Liberated Areas and the universal demand for peace and democracy across the country, and because of Chiang Kai-shek's incomplete war preparation, he found it difficult to start the civil war immediately. Instead, he devised a "peace" scheme under the direction of the United States. In August 1945, he telegramed Mao Zedong thrice, inviting the latter for peace talks in Chongqing. He calculated that, if Mao Zedong refused his invitation, he could blame the Chinese Communist Party for causing another civil war; if Mao Zedong accepted the invitation, he could use the "peace talks" to deceive the people, while gaining valuable time to prepare fully for war.

To struggle for genuine peace and also to reveal the true face of the Kuomintang that spoke of peace but actually prepared for war, the delegation of the Chinese Communist Party, led by Mao Zedong and consisting also of Zhou Enlai and Wang Ruofei, left for Chongqing for peace talks on August 28, 1945. The talk lasted 43 days, but agreement was never reached on the basic issues of the national government and army. Nevertheless, a document entitled "Minutes of the Talks Between the Kuomintang and the Communist Representatives", or the "Double Tenth Agreement", was signed on October 10, 1945. In this document, the Kuomintang was forced to recognize that "civil war must be avoided at all costs, and an independent, free, prosperous, and strong new China be created".

However, hardly had the "Double Tenth Agreement" been made public when hundreds of thousands of

Kuomintang troops moved from southeastern Shanxi and the Beiping-Hankou Railway to attack the Liberated Areas. The army and the people in the Liberated Areas counter-attacked and put out of action more than 100,000 intruders in the process. They dealt a severe blow to the Kuomintang's evil scheme of starting a civil war.

Having sensed that the time of launching a civil war had not yet arrived, Chiang Kai-shek resorted to peace deception again. On January 10, 1946, the Kuomintang signed a truce agreement with the Chinese Communist Party. But isolated attacks on the Liberated Areas continued, sometimes on a massive scale. On the day when the truce agreement was signed, the Political Consultative Conference was held in Chongqing. Through the joint effort of the Chinese Communist Party and other democratic parties, five resolutions beneficial to peace and democracy were passed. The frustrated Kuomintang sent its special agents to sabotage a meeting that was held to celebrate the victory. The agents beat and wounded more than 60 delegates, including Guo Moruo who presided over the meeting. Later, the Kuomintang agents assassinated such democratic personnel as Li Gongpu and Wen Yiduo. At the Second Plenary Session of the Kuomintang's Sixth Central Executive Committee held in March, Chiang Kai-shek openly tore into pieces the resolutions that had been passed by the Political Consultative Conference. In June, believing that preparation for war was now complete and the right time had arrived, he unilaterally abrogated the truce agreement in toto and launched an all-out civil war.

Defeat of Chiang's Attacks. On June 26, 1946, the Kuomintang troops began to attack the Liberated Areas on all fronts, thus precipitating a civil war of unprecedented scale in all of China's history.

At the beginning of the civil war, the Kuomintang had an army of 4.3 million men and ruled a population of 300 million. It controlled the large cities and most lines of communication and transportation. It possessed all the armaments surrendered to it by one million Japanese troops; it had also the military and financial support of the Americans. The Chinese People's Liberation Army,[1] on the other hand, had only 1.2 million men. It was in fact an army equipped with "millet plus rifles". It enjoyed no foreign assistance. The Liberated Areas consisted mostly of villages, with a population of about 100 million. With a difference in strength like this, there was no wonder that the Kuomintang should be so arrogant as to announce that it would destroy the People's Liberation Army in a period of three to six months.

Facing the attack by a superior enemy, the Chinese Communist Party decided to concentrate a superior force to destroy the enemy's effective strength. It did not make the holding or seizing of a city or other place its main objective. Politically, it strove to form a united front among all the people for opposition to U.S. imperialism and Chiang Kai-shek. Because of the right policy adopted by the Chinese Communist Party, the People's Liberation Army became stronger and stronger as it continued to fight and, in the first eight months of the nationwide civil war, destroyed 700,000 of the enemy's troops. In March 1947, the Kuomintang stopped its of-

---

[1] The Eighth Route Army, the New Fourth Army and other anti-Japanese armed units led by the Chinese Communist Party were designated as the Chinese People's Liberation Army during the period of the Third Revolutionary Civil War.

fensive on all fronts and concentrated its attack on the Liberated Areas in Shandong and northern Shaanxi. Once again, the People's Liberation Army beat back the intruders.

The Kuomintang policy of selling out the country, practising dictatorship, and engaging in civil war caused an upsurge of the people's democratic movement. In December 1946, 500,000 students across the nation staged strikes and demonstrations to protest an American soldier's raping of a Beijing University student. They demanded that the United States withdraw its troops from China and stop interfering with China's internal affairs. Beginning in May 1947, students of more than 60 cities demonstrated for the patriotic and democratic movement, as they opposed hunger, civil war, and persecution. In 29 cities, including Shanghai and Tianjin, 3.2 million workers participated in the movement by staging strikes and demonstrations in the year 1947. In that year, the peasant movement spread to 17 provinces, and peasants who participated in armed uprisings reached one million. On February 28, 1947, people of various nationalities in Taiwan launched massive armed uprisings and succeeded in controlling large areas, only to be brutally crushed by the Kuomintang. The people's democratic movement in the Kuomintang-controlled areas became a second front in the war against Chiang Kai-shek's reactionary rule. Now he found himself caught in the dragnet of the whole people.

Land Reform in Liberated Areas and Expansion of People's Democratic United Front. To satisfy the land demand by the peasants, the Chinese Communist Party, in May 1946, stated that the policy of rent and interest reduction, that had been carried out during the anti-

Japanese war, would be changed to a policy of confiscation of land from the landlord class and its redistribution among the peasants. In September 1947, the "Outline of the Agrarian Law of China" was made public. It stipulated that the land system of feudal and semi-feudal exploitation was to be abolished, and the land system incorporating the concept of "land to the tillers" would take its place; and that land was to be confiscated from landlords without compensation, for equitable redistribution among the rural population. Through the land reform, over 100 million peasants in the Liberated Areas received land, and they were now more than willing to support the People's Liberation Army or join the army themselves. Their enthusiasm was a guarantee for an early victory of the People's Liberation War.

In October 1947, the People's Liberation Army issued a manifesto calling upon the people to "overthrow Chiang Kai-shek and liberate all China". It put forward this political programme: "Unite workers, peasants, soldiers, intellectuals and businessmen, all oppressed classes, all people's organizations, democratic parties, minority nationalities, overseas Chinese and other patriots; form a national united front; overthrow the dictatorial Chiang Kai-shek government; and establish a democratic coalition government".[1] In December, the Chinese Communist Party specified three key points of its economic policy: (1) confiscate land from the feudal landlords and redistribute it among the peasants; (2) confiscate monopoly capital, headed by the Four Big Families of Chiang Kai-shek, Song Ziwen, Kong Xiangxi and Chen Lifu, and turn it over to the new-democratic state; and (3) protect

---

[1] "Manifesto of the Chinese People's Liberation Army", *Selected Works of Mao Zedong*, FLP, Beijing, 1977, Vol. IV, p. 150.

the industry and commerce of the national bourgeoisie. The new policy received wide support of the masses. The various democratic parties, responding to the Communist call, expressed their desire to co-operate. The people's democratic united front, under the leadership of the Chinese Communist Party, was thus expanded as never before.

Liberation of the Mainland. From June to September 1947, the People's Liberation Army launched a nationwide offensive, and the main battlefields had by this time moved to the Kuomintang-controlled areas. It captured many heavily defended cities and destroyed much of the enemy's effective strength.

Beginning in August 1948, the People's Liberation Army conducted three campaigns — the Liaoxi-Shenyang, the Beiping-Tianjin, and the Huai-Hai — that were known all over the world. These lasted altogether 142 days, during which 1.54 million of the enemy's troops were destroyed. In terms of scale, or the number of enemies destroyed, the three campaigns were unprecedented in the war annals of China and seldom known in those of the world. As a result, all of northeast China, most of north China and the east and central China areas north of the Changjiang River were liberated. Nearly all of Chiang Kai-shek's best troops were wiped out.

On the eve of the nationwide victory, the Chinese Communist Party, in March 1949, held the Second Plenary Session of its Seventh Central Committee at Xibaipo Village, Pingshan County, Hebei Province, during which Mao Zedong made an important report. The session decided on the basic policies regarding the speedy attainment of a nationwide victory and the construction of a new China after the victory. After the meeting, the

Central Committee of the Chinese Communist Party and
the headquarters of the People's Liberation Army all
moved to Beiping. Meanwhile, leaders of the democratic
parties and other democratic personnel also journeyed to
Beiping.

On January 1, 1949, Chiang Kai-shek issued a hypo-
critical declaration, ostensibly to seek peace. Actually,
he wanted to gain some breathing time so as to stage a
comeback. In connection with this declaration, Mao Zedong, on January 14, made public his viewpoint on the
current situation. He proposed eight conditions for se-
curing real peace, including punishment of war criminals.
Once his mask was smashed, Chiang Kai-shek "retired"
from his presidency on January 21, and vice-president Li
Zongren came to the fore. With the Communist Party's
eight conditions as the basis, the Kuomintang and the
Communist Party held peace talks which began in Beiping on April 1. On April 15, delegates of the two sides
drew up the final revised version of an "Agreement on
Domestic Peace". On April 20, Li Zongren refused to
sign the document, and the Kuomintang's peace offensive
collapsed in the end.

The second day, one million People's Liberation
Army men began to cross the Changjiang River and
march southward. On April 23, it captured Nanjing, the
centre of Chiang Kai-shek's reactionary rule, thus
ending the Kuomintang regime for good. Then, like
autumn wind sweeping fallen leaves, the people's army
pursued the remnants of the Kuomintang army and put
them out of action. From July 1946 to June 1950, it
destroyed a total of 8.07 million Kuomintang troops.
Other than Tibet (which was peacefully liberated in

1951), Taiwan, and some islands along the coast, all of China was liberated. The Chinese people won the Third Revolutionary Civil War.

Establishment of the People's Republic. On September 21, 1949, the Chinese People's Political Consultative Conference held its First Plenary Session in Beiping. It was attended by 662 delegates representing the various revolutionary classes, democratic parties, people's organizations and nationalities, and overseas Chinese. Exercising the powers and functions of the National People's Congress, the conference passed "The Common Program of the Chinese People's Political Consultative Conference" which served as a provisional constitution. It proclaimed the establishment of the People's Republic of China, a people's democratic dictatorship led by the working class and based upon the alliance between workers and peasants. Beiping, renamed Beijing, was to be the capital of the new China. The conference elected Mao Zedong as Chairman of the Central People's Government. The Vice-Chairmen it elected included Zhu De, Liu Shaoqi, Soong Ching Ling, Li Jishen, and Zhang Lan. Later, the Central People's Government Council held its first meeting and appointed Zhou Enlai to be Premier of the Government Administration Council and concurrently Minister of Foreign Affairs.

On October 1, 1949, 300,000 citizens gathered on the Tiananmen Square, Beijing, to attend the ceremony that marked the formal beginning of a new nation. Chairman Mao Zedong solemnly announced that the People's Republic of China had been established. One quarter of the world's population had stood up, and Chinese history entered a new period.

6. CONTEMPORARY CULTURE

Characteristics. The change in Chinese culture after
the May Fourth Movement was even more pronounced
than the change after the Opium War. The change after
the Opium War was marked by the successful, though
partially, onslaught of the bourgeoisie against the feudal
culture. Writers like Gong Zizhen and Wei Yuan opposed feudal thought; Yan Fu introduced Western
theories; and Wu Jianren wrote Western-style novels.
Of particular significance were, of course, the political
theories advanced by the bourgeois revolutionaries headed by Sun Yat-sen. Even in the field of natural sciences
and technology, the accomplishments were meant to meet
the demand of the bourgeoisie which they served. The
new culture after the Opium War, however, did not win
any great victory over feudal culture, and obviously it
could not check the cultural aggression by the imperialists. The situation was totally different after the May
Fourth Movement. With the appearance of the Chinese
proletariat and the Chinese Communist Party on the
political stage, Marxism began to arm the cultural war-
riors. A new cultural army, thus created, was able to
unite with all possible allies to launch a brave and heroic
attack against its imperialist and feudal foe. "This new
force," said Mao Zedong, "has made great strides in the
domain of the social sciences and of the arts and letters,
whether of philosophy, economics, political science, military science, history, literature or art. . . ."[1]

Flowering of New Literature. After the May
Fourth Movement, the new literature was able to over-

---

[1] "On New Democracy", *Selected Works of Mao Zedong*,
FLP, Beijing, 1975, Vol. II, p. 372.

come many difficulties to become exuberant and flourishing. Vernacular Chinese replaced literary Chinese as
the popular medium, and many literary and art societies,
such as the Literature Study Society and Creation
Society, came into existence. Meanwhile, new magazines of literature, such as *Novels Monthly* and *Creation
Weekly,* mushroomed. With the passage of time, Marxism exercised more and more influence on the new literature. In March 1930, the League of Left-Wing
Writers was established in Shanghai under the leadership of the Chinese Communist Party. Lu Xun, a leader
of the league, trained and led many Left-wing writers
to fight against the counter-revolutionary cultural "encirclement and suppression" campaigns launched by the
Kuomintang government. He and his colleagues decisively defeated their enemies. In this fierce battle, Lu
Xun proved to be a great standard-bearer of the cultural
revolution of China. He used his essays as weapons to
attack the imperialists and the Kuomintang and to sing
the glory of the proletarian revolution. He wrote many
such essays which educated the Chinese people as well
as struck effectively against the enemy.

Guo Moruo (1892-1978) and Mao Dun (1896-1981)
were another two of the greatest architects of modern
Chinese literature. In his collection of poems, *The God-
desses,* Guo Moruo exhibits the uncompromising fighting
spirit of anti-feudalism. The poems, which unequivo-
cally condemn the ugliness of the old world as they enthusiastically praise the beauty of the new one, provided
courage and hope for youths at that time. In the novel
Midnight, one of his representative works, Mao Dun
describes vividly the kind of life the comprador and national bourgeoisie led and points out that a semi-colonial

and semi-feudal society like China could not take the capitalist road. The novel also describes the worker and peasant movements and the dark side of the old society.

In the Liberated Areas, revolutionary literature also made great strides. In May 1942, Mao Zedong made public his *Talks at the Yan'an Forum on Literature and Art,* in which he pointed out, clearly and correctly, that literature must serve the workers, peasants, and soldiers. After the talks, literary and art workers went among the peasants, workers, and soldiers. As a result, they were able to create works welcomed by the masses. Among these works were *The White-Haired Girl* (an opera written collectively), *Wang Gui and Li Xiangxiang* (a narrative poem by Li Ji), *The Marriage of Young Blacky, Rhymes of Li Youcai, Changes in Li Village* (all three by Zhao Shuli), *The Sun Shines Over the Sanggan River* (by Ding Ling), and *The Hurricane* (by Zhou Libo). All these works were well-known and representative.

Achievements in Historiography. After the May Fourth Movement, Marxism slowly established its dominance in historical studies. Li Dazhao laid the foundation for the Marxist interpretation of history, and his *Essentials of Historiography,* published in 1924, was the first book in China that systematically and comprehensively presented a Marxist viewpoint.

From 1927 to 1937, the debate on three major issues — the nature of Chinese society, the periodization of Chinese history and the nature of Chinese rural society — dominated the academic scene. The practical significance of this debate was that analysis of the nature of Chinese society from a historical as well as a contemporary point of view would help to determine the character and task of the Chinese revolution, to pinpoint its

enemies, to specify the forces it had to rely on, and to
outline the future that was in store for it. The debate
made more and more people realize that China then was
a semi-colonial and semi-feudal society and that the task
of the Chinese revolution was anti-imperialism and anti-
feudalism. The debate demonstrated the power of
Marxist historiography and its importance for revolutionary practice. In 1930, Guo Moruo published *A Study of
Ancient Chinese Society*, in which he pointed out that the
development of Chinese history conformed to the general
law of the historical development of human society as a
whole. He also discussed the inevitable future of China's
historical development. His book, like Li Dazhao's
Essentials of Historiography, was a first attempt to
examine Chinese history from a Marxist point of view.

Many outstanding works on history emerged during
the anti-Japanese war and the People's War of Liberation
that followed. Among them were *The Age of Bronze*
and *Ten Criticisms* by Guo Moruo, *An Outline General
History of China* by Fan Wenlan, *A Concise General
History of China* by Lü Zhenyu, *Outline of Chinese His-
tory* by Jian Bozan, *Imperialism and Chinese Politics* by
Hu Sheng, and three works by Hou Wailu, namely, *A
History of Ancient Chinese Philosophy*, *A History of
Modern Chinese Philosophy*, and *A History of Ancient
Chinese Society*. All of these are representative works
of Marxist historiography.

The Chinese Communist Party has always emphasized the importance of studying history. In his famous
article, "Reform Our Study," Mao Zedong lists history,
theory, and current conditions as three principal subjects
of study. He proposes that we should accept the cultural heritage of China critically, absorbing what is best

and discarding the dross. During the War of Resistance Against Japan, he said emphatically that the study of history was a prerequisite to the winning of victory by a political party that was leading a great revolutionary movement.

Development of Marxism. Guided by Marxism, all aspects of contemporary Chinese culture — literature, the arts, or social sciences — acquired a new, refreshing outlook. After the May Fourth Movement, Marxism not only received extensive recognition and application but also experienced new development in China. This meant the combination of the universal truth of Marxism with the revolutionary practice of China, a combination that led to the formation of Mao Zedong Thought — a theoretical system capable of achieving the liberation of semicolonial and semi-feudal China in the era of imperialism. Mao Zedong Thought resulted not only from the creative work of Mao Zedong himself, but also from the concentration of the wisdom of the whole Chinese Communist Party and all the Chinese people. During the period of the new-democratic revolution, Mao Zedong Thought guided the Chinese people from one victory to another. Since the establishment of the People's Republic, it has served, and will continue to serve, as a powerful guide to them.

Appendix:

Chronological Table of Chinese History

Primitive Society	Remote antiquity-4,000 years ago
Slave Society	Around 21st century-476 B.C.
Xia	Around 21st-16th century B.C.
Shang	Around 16th-11th century B.C.
Western Zhou	Around 11th century-770 B.C.
Spring and Autumn Period	770-476 B.C.
Feudal Society	475 B.C.-A.D. 1840
Warring States Period	475-221 B.C.
Qin	221-207 B.C.
Western Han	206 B.C.-A.D. 24
Eastern Han	25-220
Three Kingdoms	220-280
Wei	220-265
Shu	221-263
Wu	229-280
Western Jin	265-316
Eastern Jin	317-420

Southern and Northern Dynasties	420-589
Southern Dynasties	420-589
Song	420-479
Qi	479-502
Liang	502-557
Chen	557-589
Northern Dynasties	386-581
Northern Wei	386-534
Eastern Wei	534-550
Western Wei	535-557
Northern Qi	550-577
Northern Zhou	557-581
Sui	581-618
Tang	618-907
Five Dynasties	907-960
Song (Northern and Southern)	960-1279
Liao	916-1125
Western Xia	1038-1227
Kin	1115-1234
Yuan	1271-1368
Ming	1368-1644
Qing	1644-1911

历　史

《中国手册》编辑委员会编

*

外文出版社出版
（中国北京百万庄路24号）
外文印刷厂印刷
中国国际书店发行
（北京399信箱）
1982（32开）第一版
编号：（英）17050—162
00145
17—E—1662P